The Big Thicket
An Ecological Reevaluation

Pete A. Y. Gunter

Foreword by
Bob Armstrong

Photography by
Roy Hamric

University of North Texas Press

Printed in the United States of America

1 2 3 4 5 6 7 8 9 10

Requests for permission to reproduce material from this work should be
sent to:

Permissions
University of North Texas Press
Post Office Box 13856
Denton, Texas 76203-3856

This book is printed on recycled, acid free paper.

The paper used in this book meets the minimum requirements of the
American National Standard for Permanence of Paper for Printed Library
materials, Z39.48.1984.

Library of Congress Cataloging-in-Publication Data

Gunter, P. A. Y. (Pete Addison Y.), 1936–
    The Big Thicket : an ecological reevaluation / Pete A.Y. Gunter ;
foreword by Bob Armstrong ; photography by Roy Hamric.
        p.   cm. — (Philosophy and the environment series ; v. 2)
    Includes bibliographical references (p.   ) and index.
    ISBN 0-929398-52-1 : $14.95
    1. Big Thicket National Preserve (Tex.)—Guidebooks.
    2. Ecology—Texas—Big Thicket National Preserve—Guidebooks.
I. Title. II. Series.
F392.H37G82   1993
333.95'09764'15—dc20   93-23054
                                                                CIP

To Lance Rosier
and
Senator Ralph Yarborough

Contents

Foreword

A recent poll of Americans showed that eight out of ten of us now consider ourselves to be environmentalists. It would be interesting to see how that poll would have looked at the various stages of government action on the Big Thicket Preserve. If you believe, as I do, that politicians read polls, then an eighty percent environmentalist constituency should have made a few things happen sooner or better. The fact that things happened at all is a testimony to the persistence and vision of many people.

While his name does not appear in the text of this book or in the halls of Congress as a bill author, I would like to make the point that this book's author, Pete Gunter, had as much to do with the final outcome as anyone.

I first entered the Thicket in the presence of Archer`Fullingim, irrascible editor of the *Kountze News,* for years a fierce voice crying against the imminent loss of the Thicket. It was awesome. To be there with him, to hear him order me to "Look up and listen. In here you can hear the Holy Ghost," were words and an image I would never forget. "And they're cuttin' it down, Boy. If we don't do something, it'll all be gone."

Looking up, I had the same feeling I've had in the magnificent cathedrals of the world, which always seem to me to be reaching for the sky and for light. Perhaps the trees in the Thicket and the cathedrals were influenced by the same Designer.

If Archer taught me to look up, Pete Gunter taught me to look down and around. His knowledge of the whole picture, from minute detail about an orchid or an insect, to the total scope of the Thicket, is a marvelous thing to behold. His dedication to the cause had to come in part from his great knowledge of its many wonders.

Pete Gunter fought the Thicket fight with the best of all tools, his knowledge. He imparted that knowledge while walking, teaching, writing and, occasionally, using my favorite method, by playing the guitar and singing.

Someone once said that it's not worth saving these places if we don't use and enjoy them. So, if you aren't in the Thicket, read this book. Better yet, take this book to the Thicket.

Bob Armstrong
(Former Texas Land Commissioner
and Former Parks and Wildlife Commissioner
for the state of Texas. Now of Washington, D.C.)

Preface

In October, 1974, a bill was signed by President Gerald R. Ford creating a Big Thicket National Preserve. The first national biological preserve in the history of the National Park Service, its creation signaled the end of a prolonged environmental struggle with roots reaching back into the 1920s. This book is an attempt to explain both the nature of that struggle and the character of the wilderness which environmentalists labored to defend. What is the Big Thicket and where is it located? Why is it unique? What is the organizing structure of the Big Thicket National Preserve? This book provides answers to all of these questions. It also looks to the future, arguing that conservation efforts in Southeast Texas' Big Thicket are not over; rather, they have just begun. Much can be done in the future, hopefully without the rancor and bitterness that have characterized conservation disputes there in the past.

Over twenty years ago this writer authored a book about the Big Thicket. The present work differs from it in many ways. Three new chapters have been added. A chapter has been deleted, chapters have been collapsed into single chapters, the order of passages within chapters has often been changed, and old materials have been updated. Few sentences remain that have not been rewritten, and "visuals" (photos, maps, etc.) have been redone. This is, then, essentially a new book.

It is new not only in structure, but in purpose as well. First, it attempts to carry the history of the Big Thicket forward from 1972 into the present, with a glimpse towards the future. The historical view will be as accurate as the author can make it, but it will be abbreviated. At least two master's theses and a doctoral dissertation have been written about this history without exhausting the details, and no attempt to duplicate or exceed these accounts will be attempted here. Those interested in pursuing this history in depth can read these works (which are listed at the end of this edition in the bibliography), or they can delve into the Big Thicket Archives at Lamar University in Beaumont.

A second goal of the present work is to present the Big Thicket National Preserve and nearby wilderness areas, not only as ecological gems, but as places that can be visited, studied, hiked, and canoed. The maps included in this volume contain outlines and descriptions of preserve units, hiking trails, campsites, and boat ramps, and explanations of how to get to them. That they are also accompanied by descriptions of plant growth associations, topography, and animal and plant life illustrates a basic point. This is not only a "What Is" study; it is also a "How To" book. Nothing could make its author happier than to see people pick up this book, carry it to the Thicket, and begin using it to make acquaintance with a unique, biologically rich, endlessly fascinating region of North America.

A word of caution, or rather, explanation, is called for here. I considered including an elaborate list of private campgrounds, motels, canoe rentals, and houseboat tours in the Big Thicket region. This information would have been extremely useful—at first. But as ownerships changed hands, as new campgrounds and rental operations emerged, the old ones would certainly close. Thus a list of such businesses would soon grow old and would need to be replaced several times before a new edition of this book would be called for. So I settled for pointing out that canoe rentals and houseboat tours and local museums do exist in the vicinity of the national preserve, along with motels and restaurants. For more specific information, however, the best advice is to contact the Southeast Texas Chamber of Commerce (1-409-838-6581), local chambers of commerce, Texas State Parks and Wildlife (1-512-389-4800), or the main office of the Big Thicket National Preserve (1-409-839-2689). Any of them will be glad to help you.

Many people are due thanks for their assistance in the preparation of this new edition: more than can be listed here. I would like to thank the staff and administration of the Big Thicket National Preserve in Beaumont for maps, advice, gossip, coffee, and the use of their extremely helpful library. Especially I would like to thank Superintendent Ron Switzer for many hours of extremely apt conversation. Specifically, most of the maps in this book are courtesy of the National Park Service, U. S. Department of the Interior, and Texas State Parks and Wildlife Department. Modifications to some of these maps have been made by the author. Thanks are also due to the staff of the Gray Library at Lamar University in Beaumont, for their assistance in using the Big Thicket Archive there. Nature Conservancy, Texas State Parks and Wildlife, Temple-Inland, Champion International, Louisiana Pacific, and the Governor's Office in Austin have generously donated time and information which have helped bring this book up to date. My gratitude goes out to them, but especially to Maxine Johnston, without whose hospitality, encouragement, and profound knowledge of the Thicket, this new edition would not have been completed.

Pete A. Y. Gunter

Foggy morning, Lower Thicket

1

Out of the Past

I ndians called it the Big Woods. Its hundred mile breadth formed a boundary, a kind of no-man's land, between the Caddo tribe to the north and the Bidai, Deadose, Patiri and Akokisa—the Atakapan speakers—to the south. Archaeological excavations in the region, though scarcely exhaustive, reveal surprisingly few campsites here, and those found are on high ground. This pattern supports the view that the jungle-like country was not densely settled by early Indians. Folklore has it that there were few paths through the deep forests, that Indians hunting there journeyed by canoe.

The first Europeans to settle Texas were the Spanish. Though they created missions from the Rio Grande to Louisiana, they seem to have given the Big Woods a cold shoulder. Their records tell of a vast forest between the Gulf of Mexico and their mission at Nacogdoches. Only Indians, they wrote, traveled there. As far as anyone knows, priests and soldiers did not follow them.

In the 1820s lavish Spanish land grants lured the first English-speaking pioneers to Texas. It is hard to know exactly what routes they followed. Few kept diaries or made maps. The picture which comes down to us is of wagons, blocked time and time again by dense growth and swampy soils along innumerable streams. Frustrated, the pioneers turned back and pushed west instead, either along the open coastal prairie to the south or the rolling, more broken woods to the north. Mile after mile of meandering jungle streams must have seemed like a gigantic, forbidding wilderness indeed. They called the obstacle the Big Thicket, and the name endured. For the most part the settlers avoided it; the stream of settlement divided and flowed around it, leaving it largely undisturbed.

By the middle of the nineteenth century, legends had grown up around the Big Thicket as luxuriant as its own swamps and choking undergrowth. In part the rapid growth of these legends stemmed from what was called the Neutral Ground, which bordered the region to the east. After the Louisiana Purchase the United States and Spain could not agree on a boundary between Louisiana and Texas. They did agree, however, on the existence of a neutral ground between the Arroyo Hondo on the east and the Sabine River on the west, where settlement was forbidden. Rather than remaining unpopulated, the disputed area quickly became a refuge for murderers, horse thieves, and gamblers. So lawless was the Neutral Ground that it required the presence of military forces. When the region was finally acquired by the United States in 1821, its inhabitants moved to the Big Thicket, which quickly acquired the dual aura of a wilderness refuge and a dark and dangerous place.

Stories of gangs of escaped slaves and organized bands of outlaws hung in the air around the Thicket like fog on a still fall morning. Tales of murder and mysterious disappearances were common. Sam Houston, one story runs, planned to hide his army there if his attack on Santa Anna's army at San Jacinto failed. There was, according to legend, at least one huge old hollow tree for each member of his troop.

In the 1960s a sawmill hand saw strange marks on a beech tree trunk. He stopped the saws and looked closer. Carved into the smooth bark was the figure of a hanged man. In the foreground, under the hanging tree, were shapes of hogs, or perhaps cattle. No one knows who was hanged, or when. But some time, somewhere, there had been a hanging, and someone paid for his sins without the luxury of judge or jury. The green depths of the Thicket are silent; no hint tells us more.

The Big Thicket's status as a sanctuary continued throughout the nineteenth century. During the Civil War gentlemen wishing to avoid the draft hid out there in obscure places like Jayhawker Baygall, Dock Trull Hammock, Blue Hole, and Panther's Den, easily evading Confederate conscription troops. Finally a draft officer named Kaiser set a fire in the woods to burn out a camp of deserters. About what actually happened there are as many stories as there are tellers. Some insist that not a single conscientious objector was hurt; others claim that several "slackers" were killed. What is certain is that for over eighty years nothing would grow on the scorched one hundred acres, which came to be known as Kaiser's Burnout. As late as the First and Second World Wars, descendants of some original Civil War holdouts hid successfully in local swamps, evading conscription.

The earlier Indians—the Bidai and Deadose and their kin— disappeared from Southeast Texas, victims of the white man's diseases, and of innumerable disruptions of their tribal lives. Their place was taken by remnants of southeastern Indian tribes, chiefly the Alabamas and the Coushattas. Like other members of the Creek confederacy, the Alabamas and Coushattas had a long history of confrontation with the white man. The Alabama River and the state of Alabama were named for the Alabama Indians, whom the French first discovered living in villages at the junction of the Coosa and Talapoosa Rivers. The Alabamas fought a long, bloody war with the French, yet ended by making an alliance with them. When the French withdrew to Louisiana in 1763 the Alabamas and Coushattas followed, settling temporarily in the "Cajun Country" around Opelousas. By 1800 they were again moving, drifting into Texas where they forged a brief, highly elastic alliance with the Spanish. As H. N. Martin tells it:

> Dr. John Sibley, the American agent in Nachitoches, Louisiana, also realized the importance of influencing the border Indians. His trading post was a popular gathering point for the Indians in the area. Here the Alabamas and other tribes received gifts and expressed loyalty to the Americans. Then, at the first opportunity, they would travel to Nacogdoches for

Spanish gifts and friendship. The Alabamas apparently understood that the Spanish and the Americans were engaged in a tug-of-war for their loyalty, and the Indians capitalized on this conflict in accordance with the opportunities that came their way.

The Indians knew very well, by sad experience, the futility of war with the ever-numerous white man. Drifting west ahead of the tide of European settlement, they struggled to retain their independence by playing one side against the other. When the southern woodlands halted at the edge of the Texas prairies they halted too, using diplomacy to win redress.

Redress was scarce. In 1840 the Republic of Texas granted the Alabamas 8854 acres (two leagues) in Tyler County. They were soon evicted by angry white settlers, however. In 1854 they were ceded 1110.7 acres, but in 1858 the state of Texas attempted to move them farther west. The tribe's chiefs explored the proposed reservation but refused to move. The Lower Brazos Reserve seemed to them a dismal place compared with Polk County's green piney hills. Besides, there was reason to fear for the tribe's safety on the new reservation. In December, 1858, a group of Texans entered the Brazos Reserve and slaughtered a sleeping camp of peaceful Anadarko and Caddo Indians. Hardin R. Runnels, Texas' governor at the time, relented, refusing to expose the Alabamas to casual slaughter. They were allowed to remain in the Thicket. Fate, for a change, was on their side.

The Coushattas (or Koasati), like the Alabamas, were Creeks. Both had fought the French. Both had moved west. Both had settled in East Texas, where they retained close contact. A legend tells that the Alabamas and Coushattas emerged from the earth on two sides of a great tree and settled there in two groups. Their languages differ, but are mutually comprehensible. The settlers, as was always the case in their view of Indians, drew few distinctions between them.

By 1830 the Alabamas had reached the peak of their development in Texas. Their three villages in Polk County had a total population of 600. Farming, hunting, and trading had made them prosperous. Within ten years, however, village life deteriorated as settlers began taking their lands. The inhabitants of two of the original villages (Long King Village and Batisse Village) were compelled either to wander the land, subject to eviction by white owners, or to live at the remaining settlement (Colita's Village, north of present-day Romayor). In 1840 the Republic of Texas granted the Coushattas two leagues of land, but by the time they were surveyed white men had already seized them. In 1859 most of the Coushattas were allowed to settle with the Alabamas. In 1885 the State of Texas granted the Coushattas 665 acres. Since suitable reservation land no longer existed in Polk County, however, this benefaction was meaningless. In 1906 the last free Coushattas were transported to the Alabama reservation.

Poverty—sad, and sadly predictable—followed. The two tribes had no training in large-scale agriculture, which the sandy loams of their reservation would not in any case have supported. Their acreage was too small to support them by timbering, and besides, even in periods of intense hunger they refused to cut their timber. As a result, their timberland today contains some of the last few stands of virgin forest in the Thicket. Some of both Texas' and North America's biggest trees in their species have been found in the rich bottomlands of the Alabama and Coushatta reservation.

Early on, the white man sent representatives of his churches to the reservation to teach the Indians "decency." Under the joint onslaught of an alien religion and poverty, Indian culture began to disintegrate as the Indian village sank into torpor. By 1920 the condition of the Alabamas and Coushattas had declined so fully that the State of Texas became moved to "do something for them." In 1928 Texas, using federal funds, purchased 3071 acres of additional land for them. Most accounts of this benefaction fail to note that the land was first cleared of valuable timber before being bestowed. Between 1928 and 1933, seventy-two tin-roofed shacks were constructed "to get the Indians out of their log cabins." Alabamas and Coushattas claim today that as many as half the members of their tribes died of starvation on the reservation. Probably no one will know for certain. The dead do not speak, and the reservation's administrators deny the claim.

Not all of the Thicket was lumbermen's country. In the original wilderness were prairies alive with wild horses and longhorn cattle, canebrakes miles in length, flower-carpeted meadows, grassy savannahs where horseback settlers hunted wild hogs, swamps too remote to timber and lowlands which, if carefully tilled, would bring in a cotton crop. But for all this diversity the main source of change was to be then, as it still is, the lumber industry.

The first serious timbering in the region took place in the years 1850-60. Most of the trees cut in this decade were floated down the Neches and the Sabine Rivers. During the Civil War the East Texas Railroad was dismantled and fed into the Confederate war effort, and no new railroad was built into the region until years afterwards. Not until the 1880s did railroads open the Big Thicket to logging, and these—the Trinity and Sabine, the Houston-East-and-West-Texas, the Sabine and East Texas—concentrated on the wilderness's western reaches. In the eastern Thicket, railroad building did not begin until the 1890s. Throughout, the pattern was the same. Shorter "trunk" lines branched out from the main railroad lines so that the entire region became a network of tracks.

The process was efficient, and complete. Eventually every stand of trees, no matter how remote, would be discovered by the railroad and quickly felled. Then the tracks would be taken up and put down elsewhere. One searches in vain for a single big tree saved, a last grove of virgin beech or magnolia bypassed, or even a handful of pines left to reseed the surrounding rubble. When the lumber companies timbered they took every tree that could be sold, and left only wreckage.

With the virtue of hindsight we can now point out that if even a single acre of Thicket had been left uncut for every ten thousand timbered, those scattered plots would today contain trees of incredible size and beauty. We could point out that the economic loss from this procedure would have been negligible. The mentality of the times, however, left little room for "use-

less" speculation. The forests fell. And some men—a few—
became rich.

Not surprisingly, settlers did not always love lumber companies. A glance over area maps will show many burned places
in the forest (Old Hat Burnout, Dunnie Burnout) unrelated to
Captain Kaiser. Some of these mark a hunter's attempt to smoke
out a bear. Others witness a settler's revenge against a lumber
company which had seized his land. The full story of land
acquisition by early lumbermen remains untold. With the aid of
a powerful infusion of Northern capital, lumbermen took advantage of Texas' "use and possession" laws to seize lands that had
been in settlers' families, often for generations. Usually the
forest was felled before the damage was found. Protesting
settlers were met at the courthouse by that all-time favorite, the
corporate lawyer, quoting obscure texts and promising expen-
sive court trials. Some who claim they dare not write about it
assert that most of the land owned by large lumber interests in
the Thicket was stolen, pure and simple. Perhaps that is an
exaggeration, but even those who hold it is believe the settlers
might have won their case if they had stuck together. Unfortunately, their native individualism made it virtually impossible
to do so.

Easily the most famous lumber baron was John Henry
Kirby. Besides owning several million acres of East Texas piney
woods, Kirby by 1906 operated twelve different sawmills (at
Evadale, Call, Bronson, Woodville, Roganville, Bessmay,
Browndell, Fuqua, Kirbyville, Mobile and Beaumont) which
churned out 1,445,000 board feet of lumber per day.

Never have men so quickly and ruthlessly cut a woodland
as they slashed the southern pine forests. Labor was cheap, the
land flat to gently rolling, the weather mild. The southern
lumber baron pushed "cut and get out" policies to unheard-of
extremes. Oddly, little lore emerged from this massive transformation. The northwestern lumberjack has no counterpart in
the mythology of the Lone Star State. Compared to the cowboy,
the oilfield roughneck, or the backwoods bear hunter, the East
Texas lumber worker appears nearly as drab a character as the
southern mill worker he partially resembles, constantly in debt

to the company store, bound to the region in which he, his wife, and children were born.

From the First World War through the 1930s, labor unrest beset the East Texas pineries. John Henry Kirby's approach to his workers was harsh but eloquent:

> I am talking for the man who has a wife and babies at home, the man who perhaps, has been visited by misfortune, the man who may not be a good manager, the man whose meal barrel is not full and who could not stand a shutdown. It is in his behalf that I would ask his fellow laborers not to push upon him conditions that will destroy him and bring tears to the cheek of his good wife, anxiety to both their hearts and distress and hunger to the little ones who toddle about their home.

No one could say that Kirby did not love children. He would close his mills immediately, he insisted, if the Brotherhood of Timber Workers were to make demands on lumber operators—any demands at all. Given the isolation and relative poverty of company towns, the South's ingrained paternalism, the friction between white and black workers, the upshot was not surprising. Unionism was slow to enter the piney woods. Salaries, living conditions, and educational levels of its workers lagged behind those of workers in other parts of the country. Company towns and company-owned counties have had a lasting influence on East Texas politics. For example, sixty-five percent of the land in Hardin County and eighty percent in Tyler County are company owned. Maps of counties with low per capita income show considerable overlap with counties in which lumber companies are the largest employers.

In the 1880s and 90s the Thicket became renowned not for its timber or for its status as a sanctuary but for its epic bear hunts. America's most famous bear hunter, Ben Lilly, came to the Big Thicket before trekking west to the last frontiers of the Rocky Mountains. Lilly claimed that he bagged his 118th bear in the Thicket—one of the largest black bears ever killed in North America. Old settlers used to talk about how Lilly could find his way in even the densest woods or how he could shinny full speed to the top of a tree or jump flatfooted out of a barrel.

Incongruously, as the last of the big bear hunts took place, the Thicket region became the scene of an oil boom. The first gusher was drilled in 1900 at Spindletop, south of Beaumont; soon after, strikes at Sour Lake (1901), Saratoga (1903), and Batson (1904) transformed once isolated villages into roaring boomtowns knee-deep in mud, drilling rigs, tent saloons and tough men from the four corners of the world.

It is not that oil was anything new to the Big Thicket, whose southmost reaches had more than their share of salt domes, warm sulphur springs, and oil seeps. Indians had long used surface seep oil in the region as medicine, and pioneers regularly shared tales of Indian cures and secret oil springs. It was not unusual for settlers to set their hogs free in the woods only to find them returning covered with black, viscous fluid from tail to snout. The settlers soon followed their hogs to the oil seeps and bottled the contents as medicine.

One of Texas' first oil wells was drilled in 1869 at Saratoga. The process was subtle and very sophisticated. A pine tree was "topped" and a second pine tree trunk was cantilevered over it with a weight on one end. The weight, acting like one side of a seesaw, was dropped onto the oil pipe, driving it into the ground: exactly as a hammer drives a nail. When a pipe was driven in, a new length was added and hammering started again. The result was not a success, producing less than a barrel a day. Like the timbering of the Thicket, an early oil boom was forestalled for thirty years by a stroke of chance.

Oil interests—certainly in the early years—have taken even less interest in preserving ecological balance than the lumbermen who preceded them. In the Thicket, oil- and saltwater-overflow from wells and sludge pits has killed big cypress trees along creeks and marshes and destroyed the nesting places of countless water birds. From the air it is easy to see still-standing dead trees down miles of meandering bayou, acres of still-barren sandy clay in now aging oilfields, half grown brush—

some dead grey, some green—around decaying oil tanks and abandoned wells. No one has ever made a map of oilfield destruction in the Big Thicket, but it would make a large, depressing tableau.

Not every transformation of the Thicket by oil companies can be chalked up to their neglect. A case in point is in the old Sour Lake oilfield, the Texas Company's Fee No. 4603, Brooks Subdivision, to be exact. It began October 7, 1929. Ordinary events gave notice that something out of the ordinary was about to take place: two wells that had been producing oil began to pump water. The next morning workers on a "bull gang" noticed something else. A place a hundred feet away "wasn't where it used to be." The ground had sunk slightly, and was starting to settle.

At first the depression was barely noticeable. An area the size of a suburban lot subsided slowly, as if pulled by an invisible string. Apprehensively, the crew moved the derrick and equipment away. Water quickly filled the low place as trees and brush on the spot began to disappear. By sundown good-sized trees had disappeared, standing upright. As the crater widened it attracted water from a nearby creek. Huge fissures at its edges pointed towards adjacent oil storage tanks. A recent well producing 250 barrels a day suddenly stopped.

Oilmen looked on in awe, hypnotized by the relentless collapse. By the third day the sink reached 140 feet (nearly one hundred feet below sea level) and stretched across nearly fifteen acres. Then, as suddenly as it began, the subsidence stopped, leaving in its wake thirty-five failed wells and a small acid lake. Only one well, Gilbert 38 just west of the sink, was improved. Pumping ten barrels a day, it spurted suddenly to 250. Production was never restored on the other thirty-five.

For a week, as journalists, curiosity seekers and oilfield workers crowded its edges, the sink was front page news. Half a dozen theories were created to explain it. The subsidence was caused by "local blasting to locate salt domes," by "changing cap rock formations and oil sands," by "removal of seventy-three million barrels of oil over the last quarter century" by "removal of salt by oil well drilling." In a paper read to the American

Institute of Mining Engineers, Dr. E. H. Sellars suggested that underlying salt was probably the cause but that no one would ever know for sure. Nearby Sour Lake (the body of water, not the town) was probably formed the same way; but that was long before anyone ever thought of drilling there. Meanwhile the crater remained, a dead sea gradually filling in, another enigma for Thicket folk to ponder.

The oil boom vanished even more quickly than the lumber railroads and the lumber mills. Small towns faded back into obscurity as oil field workers left. Even the trains ran less often. The Big Thicket fell into a sleep which lasted nearly forty years.

Settler's Cabin

2

Mapping a Cornucopia

Those who go to the Big Thicket today will not find backwoodsmen in coonskin caps. There are too many highways, too many clearcuts, too many pipeline right-of-ways and 7-11s. True, off the gravel roads that turn into dirt roads and then into tiretracks through tall grass, you may still find cabins where electricity is rejected in favor of coal oil lamps and a way of living which remains little different from that of nineteenth-century pioneers. These, however, are now very few. Trailers, white frame houses, even brick subdivision ranchstyles are far more likely. Today the old-time settler fights a losing battle with the backhoe, the bulldozer, and the power line right of way—and with something still more nebulous, more insidious, which undermines old ways of seeing things.

But neither will today's visitors find simply a barren, pillaged, biologically impoverished land. If what has been said so far has made it appear that little is left but a forest of stumps between oilfield scars, this is misleading. It is a tribute to the richness of the region that the Big Thicket, though reduced and fragmented, retains today a distinctive biological identity. This identity is particularly evident in lands too remote or too swampy to timber at a profit or in plots long entangled in litigation. It is evident also in second-growth forests which have so far escaped clearcutting and in which the region's phenomenal growth rate has produced forests approaching the Thicket's earlier botanical exuberance.

There thus remains much in the area that is still worth saving, including what has so far actually been saved. Before discussing what merits saving, or detailing the still-intense struggle to save it, the first order of business is to define the Big Thicket and its significance. What is there about this region that so profoundly interests the botanist, the hiker, the bird expert? What is there that merits such a long-standing—and complex—controversy? The answers to these questions are as interesting and as many-sided as the Thicket itself.

The settlers in Southeast Texas knew they had stumbled onto something different. "You can find anything in the Thicket," they quipped, "from a cricket to an elephant." Though no one has yet sighted an elephant there, the settlers said more than they knew. It really is no exaggeration to say that the Big Thicket is the Biological Crossroads of North America. It contains both temperate and subtropical plants and animals, along with many from the dry, treeless west. In the Thicket there are many varieties of orchids; but there are also species of sagebrush and cacti. In few other places will one find roadrunners alongside alligators, mesquite and yucca alongside cypress and water tupelo.

In spite of its uniqueness, the Big Thicket is only now beginning to receive intensive, systematic study. The first attempt at an inventory, the *Biological Survey of the East Texas Big Thicket Area*, was completed in 1938. Since then new plants and animals have entered the region and, unfortunately, others have become extinct. In an area so large and varied, moreover, the changes are difficult to trace. Even were the *Biological Survey* entirely accurate (and it is not), it is by its own admission incomplete. Research in area insect and fish life remains incomplete, and will probably produce some surprises. The same is true of its mosses, algae, lichens, molds and fungi. There is not a single category in the *Biological Survey*, from slime molds through migratory waterfowl, which can be declared final. Whoever writes about the Thicket's standing inventory had best tread warily. It is especially easy to create fiction in place of fact; it is, conversely, just as easy to deny a fact because it doesn't fit one's predilections.

On one point nearly everyone is agreed. The Thicket region contains an extraordinary diverseness, lushness and profusion of flowering plants. Most accounts are quick to point out that it contains four out of five of North America's varieties of insect-eating plants. The pitcher plant, bladderwort, sundew and butterwort grow there abundantly—though less and less so as bulldozers and brush hogs strip away habitat and drain swamps. Only Venus fly-trap is missing.

The number and richness of wildflowers are, to my mind, far more impressive than the existence there of meat-eating plants. Geyata Ajilvsgi's *Wild Flowers of the Big Thicket* describes (and includes photographs of) 475 wild flowers. The arboretum at Lamar University had built up an inventory of over 800 species from the Big Thicket before the collection was, tragically, burned. Most persons knowledgeable in botany are willing to assert that the region contains at least a thousand varieties of flowering plants. Many botanists are willing to bet that the figure will go higher.

It is against the background of these facts that one must understand the enthusiastic response to a color slide show of Big Thicket flowers, recorded in Mary Lasswell's *I'll Take Texas*.

> The list reads like the perennial section of the finest garden catalogue ever printed. . . . . I sat there in complete disbelief at what I saw: *Lobelia cardinalis* five feet high; bergamot, cream and gold. Bluebells . . . *Lilium canadense*, wild petunia, Drummond phlox, winecups; coral bean; giant trumpet vine; wild wisteria; pentstemon, a climbing form rare in most other parts of the world. Wild honeysuckle and verbena. Great blankets of gaillardia and blazing star, spider lily, yellow fringed orchid, and tway-blade, and white fragrant orchid. These are but a scant handful of the beauty native to the Thicket.

Lance Rosier, the self-trained biologist who interested so many in the region, remarked that he once counted over eighty-four varieties of wildflowers one morning in a single bend in the road near the Hardin County Consolidated School. There was no use going back to see them the next spring, he said; the place had subsequently been bulldozed.

Some of the Thicket's flowering plants are rare and endangered. Among these are *Bartonia texana* (screwstem), *E. Kornikianum* (smallhead pipewort), *Phlox nivalis texensis* (trailing phlox), *Amsonia glaberrima* (trailing catchfly), two species of sedge (*Carex fissa* and *Cyperus grayoides*), a meadow beauty (*Rhexia salicifolia*) and *Silene subciliata* (catchfly). Two flowers on the federal list of threatened species are yellow lady's slipper (*Cypripendium calceolus*) and another sedge (*Scirpus divaricatus*).

As reported by Geraldine Watson in her unpublished "Rare Plants of the Big Thicket" (early 1980s), many other species in the region, though they exist elsewhere, are rare in Texas. *Wahlenbergia emarginata* (a perennial herb) has only one known Texas location; so have *Myrica inodorus* (a variety of waxmyrtle), *Sabatia campanulata* (prairie rose gentian), and *Lupinus perennis* (a bluebonnet). Dozens of others are known in Texas only in the Big Thicket area, in only a handful of places.

Probably the strangest report of anomalous distribution in the area was the claim made in the 1930s by a biologist working on the original biological survey. He claimed to have discovered three plants in the Big Thicket whose only other known occurrence was in Iceland. The scientist is long deceased, and efforts to find out which species he had in mind have proved fruitless. Conceivably the claim is valid. But the ties between Iceland and the Big Thicket seem tenuous enough.

Equally interesting are flowering plants known to exist elsewhere in the Lone Star State which turn up in the Thicket though they were until recently not supposed to exist there. Among these are ten species of wildflowers native to West Texas, one native to the South Texas prairies, and some even to the southwestern deserts. These continue to crop up, much to the surprise of botanists. Recently a gourd vine which flourishes along Hill Country limestone creeks was found at the confluence of Menard Creek and the Trinity River.

Though flowers are found blooming in the region in every month of the year, spring produces the most abundant show. In deep woods, dogwood and magnolia burst into flower. Wild azalea, smoketree, orchids and redbud flower overnight, spangling the new green of April grass and trees with pink, white, and red. Ferns unfurl in deep creekbottoms, honeysuckle begins its creep along fence lines. Colored mushrooms fleck the dull forest floor.

It comes as a shock to most people to hear that the Thicket's carpet of flowers contains orchids. It should come as even more of a surprise to discover that there are so many kinds. Of the forty-one orchids listed as being in Texas by the New York Botanical Gardens, thirty-one (that is, seventy-six percent) are in the Big Thicket area. Few are as large or as striking as those in a florist shop; but many are a great deal rarer. Among these, one (already listed above), is an endangered species: the yellow lady's-slipper. Others include grass pink, spreading pogonia, wisters coral root, small green wood orchid, bog torch, whorled pogonia, and the shadowwitch. The crested coral root (*Hexalectris spicata*) was found in Texas for the first time in a Neches River swamp little more than a decade ago.

Sharing the orchids' damp habitats are a number of orchid relatives and some thirty varieties of ferns. On shaded creekbanks under deep shade the Thicket hiker is likely to run into sensitive fern, southern lady fern, water fern, and the lavish cinnamon fern. In the spring and summer he will pause to examine tree trunks and branches thick with moss and resurrection fern, which transforms from dried brown to living green in a single day of abundant rain. If fortunate, he may stumble across a species no one had thought existed in the Thicket, as happened around ten years ago with the discovery of the Florida shieldfern in the Neches River lowlands.

While wildflowers and ferns have a natural grace and beauty that attracts us, the same cannot be said of the next item on the inventory, molds and fungi. The *Biological Survey of the East Texas Big Thicket Area*, which didn't even attempt to deal with them, speculated that as many as one to two thousand species of molds and fungi might eventually be found in the area.

After nearly twenty years of field work, David P. Lewis now suggests that at least three thousand species can be found there *of the larger mushroom types alone.* Starting in the 1950s, only three mycologists (mold/fungi specialists) have worked in Southeast Texas: Harry D. Thiers, William Cibula, and David Lewis. So far—especially since the mid 1970s—several hundred new species have been discovered there.

This may not seem as dramatic as an encounter with an enraged bear or even the discovery of a new flamboyant species of orchid. But it will surely be far more important in the long run. Not only might the complex biochemistry of a mold or a fungus provide a treatment for cancer or a cure for high blood pressure or encephalitis, but it is also becoming increasingly clear that certain sorts of fungi (micorrhizal fungi) are symbiotic with the forests where they are found. This means not only that the forest shelters and nourishes the fungi, but that the fungi provide nourishment and other resources (e.g. water cycling) to the forest. If one is to have a healthy and productive forest, one must protect the soil fungi.

Some of the fungi found in the Thicket turn out to have been found elsewhere in only one or two places, some of them farther away than even Iceland. *Galerina calyptrata* Orton (that great all-time favorite) is known previously only from England; two other species are known only from sites in Trinidad and in the mountain rainforests of Venezuela. Species with jawbreaking names like *Amanita komarekensis*, *Hygrophorus cantharellus*, and *Polyphorus umbellatus*—mercifully to name only a few—are known from only one or two other locations in the world.

It has been implied here that fungi are unlovely. That is not necessarily so. The writer recalls a weekend when the national board of the Audubon Society visited the Big Thicket. Conservationists went all out to impress the visiting dignitaries. Lush fern valleys, immense old cypress trees, orchids and rarely seen orchid relatives, rare species of woodpeckers, deep baygall swamps—none of them impressed the Audubon board. But the mushrooms: the visitors could not hide their astonishment. Nowhere had they seen such a display!

[18]

Champion Cypress tree

To tell the truth, the writer was equally stunned. For all the thousands of hours he had spent in the woods, he had really never focused on mushrooms and toadstools. That day they were out in overwhelming abundance, like a rainbow: blue, copper, red-orange, brown, green, yellow, grey, black, white. These were not dull brown or gauzy grey or rotted black; they were a riot of color. And when the mushrooms got tired of growing on the ground, they played leapfrog, growing on one another. A cobalt blue mushroom grew on a white and brown "bracket fungus"; and a small yellow mushroom grew on it. You had to go far back in the woods, to leaf mulch a foot deep under heavy shade, to find them. But they were there, proving that not only orchids are beautiful.

One key to the wide variety of flowers, ferns, and fungi in the Thicket is the variety of trees that grow there. Given its image as a prairie-desert covered by mesquite and cactus, Texas is one of the last places where one would go to look for trees. The Big Thicket, however, receives between fifty and sixty inches of rain per year—a characteristic which it shares with much of Louisiana and Florida. When coupled with sandy water-storing soils, the result is as impressive as it is predictable: huge trees, some of which are the largest in their species.

The cataloging of big trees is a relatively recent practice. Begun in 1940 by the American Forestry Association, it was an attempt "to halt the tragic disappearance of America's most magnificent tree specimens." The idea has worked. "Champion" trees (i.e., the largest in their species) are now sought out and given publicity and a title. Competition to seek out and establish state and national champions has led people who once could have cared less to go far out of their way to protect local giants and near-giants. It is an exception to a rule; here the competitive spirit has had a positive effect on nature.

Championship status, of course, is not conferred in perpetuity. Old champions die, and even if they do not, new ones are commonly found to take their place. For this reason no attempt will be made to give an up-to-the-minute account of reigning tree champions of the Big Thicket. By the time this book has been in print three or four years, a third or a fourth of the champions will already have been displaced. A survey of Thicket giants completed in the early 1970s will suffice to demonstrate why the region's trees have gained such respect.

Roughly, (because this figure too is subject to change), there are one hundred and ten tree species in the Big Thicket. These are largely "overstory" trees, in contrast to the "understory" of small trees and bushes. Of these, fifty-six were registered as state champions and fifteen as national champs. These were: common crepe myrtle, black hickory, American holly, Texas honey locust, Rugel sugar maple, bluejack oak, longleaf pine, redbay, western soapberry, tree sparkleberry, sweetbay magnolia, Chinese tallow, water tupelo and yaupon. Interestingly, four of these reach record size at the far western edge of their species' distribution. Water elm, planertree, sweetbay, sugar hackberry, common sweetleaf, Allegheny chinkapin, two-winged silverbell, eastern redcedar and sugarberry in the Thicket region had formerly been national champions, but had been demoted to the status of near-champions.

In reading the list of trees from the 1938 biological survey, it is interesting to note the number of species which normally do not range as far west or south as the Thicket. The nutmeg hickory presumably grows no closer to the area than Mississippi and southern Arkansas. The rock chestnut oak is a tree of the Appalachian mountains. The speckled alder ranges no farther south than Pennsylvania and Nebraska. The Ohio buckeye's range is assumed to reach no farther than Northeast Texas, where it is an infrequent intruder from Arkansas and Oklahoma. Some of the trees cataloged by the 1938 survey must have resulted from identification errors. Among these are the wavyleaf oak (Colorado-Nebraska), the nutmeg hickory (Southern Arkansas), and the Mexican persimmon (Southwest Texas). Before we become too dogmatic about the survey and its results, however, we should take note of the discovery, in the last five years, of *Acer leucoderme* along the upper Neches River corridor. This is a maple not previously known to exist in Texas.

Before completing the list of Thicket species it will be interesting to note some real oddities. The first is a monkey colony found there in the fall of 1966. What the monkeys were doing there and whether they survived the winter is not known. A boy shot one of them and brought it to Beaumont: a full-grown squirrel monkey. He had to shoot one, he said, or no one would believe him. Just as strange as tales of lost monkey colonies is a story recounted by Dempsie Henley in *The Murder of Silence*. A friend of Henley's—a Houston businessman—was given a big black Australian wolfhound as a present. The dog did not take to suburban living, however, and the businessman finally set it free on a deserted Big Thicket road. The wolfhound loped around the car several times and then headed out into the woods. Not long afterward remote settlers reported a huge black dog seen skulking around their cabins. It was leading a wolf pack. Perhaps this explained the problems of the elderly lady who lived in the old hotel in the abandoned town of Bragg, in Hardin County. She had to start feeding her dogs indoors, she complained. When she fed them outdoors the wolves ate the dogfood off the back steps.

Not many years ago, as the author hiked the palmetto flats along Pine Island Bayou in the Thicket, he met a man riding on a pony and blowing a tin horn. The man explained that he had lost his dogs while hunting and had looked for them every day for two weeks. He had, he explained, given up hope of finding them. Perhaps they are still out there.

It has not been that long since a journalist from an Eastern newspaper reported the story that a herd of three or four dozen jackasses had been turned out into the Thicket to run wild. Conceivably the hunter's dogs are chasing the stockman's wild jackasses. If nothing else, these accounts suggest that no one should be too sure about what there is to find on a hike through the Big Thicket.

Any Thicket inventory ought to mention, in addition to orchids and dogs and mushrooms, by far the most dangerous creature there: the two-legged hairless ape. Of this species, the most spectacular are those which hide in the deep woods seeking sanctuary. The most famous of these is the Nude Man of the Big Thicket, who lived there in the 1950s. Several people had already glimpsed the man when one fine day a Mr. Sutton came across him on a lonely sand road. He was large, deeply tanned, with a long beard. He had a gun in each hand and was entirely naked. If anyone wanted to come in after him, he remarked, they would have to come in shooting. So far as is known, no one accepted the challenge, though there are stories of the subsequent capture of an escaped mental patient who had lived on wild fruits and armadillo for nine years. Whether the two hermits are the same man is—well, the facts get vague on that point.

Two decades of asking questions and plowing through old newspaper files have not, incidentally, uncovered even a hint of sightings of a "Bigfoot" or other vast hominid hiding out in the region. I report this with a certain relief. The Big Thicket with its aura of legend would, one might imagine, be a "natural" for Bigfoot or related legends. Equally, it would be a likely place for hoaxes. But no dice; so far there is not even a single wild report.

In 1938 a murderer and bank robber named Red Goleman stole a cab in Houston and headed out for his native Big Thicket. Old-timers say it was a weird sight to see Goleman at night, cutting down some back road with his roof lights glowing in blackness. A man in a cab in a wilderness is not exactly inconspicuous; but Goleman managed to hide out for three months without getting caught (or overcharging a fare, either). Not until the lawmen of both Jefferson and Hardin counties got together and cashed in on a tip was the outlaw trapped and riddled with bullets in the corncrib in back of his mother's house. For several years the corncrib was a sort of local tourist attraction, until the novelty of it wore off.

The other two-legged creatures in the Thicket are the birds. Not only are they, with few exceptions, less dangerous than man, but they are also a lot more graceful. There are around three hundred species of birds in the region. More than one hundred are year-round residents; the rest are migratory. The number of the latter is significant. The Thicket is one of the important stopping points for migrating birds along the Gulf Coast. It may be more important as a migratory haven than it is as a year-round sanctuary for rare, scarce, and otherwise interesting birds.

The number 300 may not seem impressive, unless one knows that the number of bird species in the United States is around 720; the number for Texas 540. The significance of this last figure becomes apparent when one discovers that the number for California, which has the nation's second largest species count, is only 439. Thus the Big Thicket contains more than one-third of the bird species found in the United States, and more than half of those found in Texas. Very few states— a handful—shelter as many bird species as the remaining acres of the Big Thicket.

There are birder lists and National Park Service reports and hundreds of maps of summer and winter ranges for birds of North America. But there is no official checklist of Big Thicket bird life. Olin Pettingill laments:

> Northwest of industrial Beaumont, with its factories and refineries and its oak-and-magnolia-shaded residential districts, sprawls the BIG THICKET, a wilderness area estimated to cover some two million acres. Why, considering its extent, its fascinating complexity of terrain and plant distribution, and its reputed richness in birdlife, it remains an unknown quantity ornithologically cannot be answered.

Pettingill's remarks, written in 1953, are still valid. Though the Thicket is no longer an "unknown quantity" ornithologically, much remains to be worked out in detail. What follows is in part an estimate—a mixed bag of eyewitness reports and general distribution patterns.

It is hard to imagine a woodpecker as big as a hawk. The ivory-billed woodpecker, however, achieves this distinction, if it indeed still exists. The ivory-bill, though it once ranged from the Gulf of Mexico as far north as the southern tip of Indiana and as far east as North Carolina, is now believed extinct. One of its last possible habitats is the Big Thicket, where it is reported from time to time, only to vanish when birdwatchers and photographers converge to identify it.

Two factors have determined its demise. The first is the disappearance of the virgin woodlands upon which the big woodpeckers depend. Almost as important are its size and striking appearance. At an overall body length of twenty-one inches (compared to the broadwinged hawk at eighteen, the duck hawk at nineteen, and the chicken hawk at twenty) and its flamboyant black, white, and red markings, it has evoked such names as "goodgod," "mygod," and "godamighty." It has also evoked the pride of backwoods marksmen, who have made it their favorite target.

The ivory-bill's elusiveness is fully matched by its strength and vigor. A naturalist who confined one to his hotel room in Wilmington, North Carolina, wrote:

> In less than an hour I returned, and, on opening the door he set up a distressed shout, which appeared to proceed from grief that he had been discovered in his attempts to escape. He had mounted along the side of the window, nearly as high as the ceiling, a little below which he began to break through. The bed was covered with large pieces of plaster, the lath was exposed for at least fifteen inches square, and a hole large enough to admit the fist opened to the weatherboards; so that, in less than an hour he certainly would have succeeded in making his way through.

Also a strong flyer, the ivory-bill can easily range over an area thirty to forty miles wide. This helps to explain—at least in part—why a given locale may often yield only one sighting; an hour later the big shy bird may be miles away.

In the late 1960s a grizzled backwoodsman walked into the office of *Kountze News* editor Archer Fullingim. He asked Archer if he believed there were any more of those ivory-billed birds like the ones whose pictures were in the paper. When Archer replied skeptically the man reached out and dumped a dead ivory-billed woodpecker on his desk. The editor looked on in dismay as the settler grinned. "Those birds are out at my place. They're the rarest birds in the world and I've got 'em. Ain't

nobody but me knows where they are." The man pocketed the
bird in his jacket and walked out, remarking that there were
"plenty more where that one came from." Fullingim learned
later that the man had seen no more ivory-bills. They had
deserted his land seeking, no doubt, a deeper solitude.

The last believable ivory-bill sighting of which this author
knows was reported in 1980. In 1991 there were reports from
Cuba's Oriente province of the presence of ivory-bills. Perhaps
so. But efforts at definite identification, as always, failed. As
things now stand, one is a lot less likely to see an ivory-bill than
one is to see a brontosaurus.

Would-be ivory-bill discoverers have to cope with a second
problem. If one did see the bird, they complain, skeptics would
insist it was only a pileated woodpecker. Around the turn of the
century, ornithologists were mournfully sure that pileated
woodpeckers would follow the ivory-bills into extinction. Fortunately the pileated woodpecker has managed to adapt to
cutover woodlands. Like the ivory-bill but smaller (with a body
length of nineteen inches), the pileated woodpecker is a bird of
remote, little frequented places. That it exists in the Thicket is
a tribute to that area's remaining deep woods and back country
swamps.

Four other rare birds are found in the Big Thicket: the
brown-headed nuthatch, the red-cockaded woodpecker, the
peregrine falcon, and the bald eagle. A fifth formerly claimed for
the area, Bachman's warbler, is now considered extinct. The
red-cockaded woodpecker provides a classic case of a bird
threatened by radical changes in its habitat. A comparatively
small bird at seven inches long, it sports a zebra-striped ladder
back, a black crown and a large white face patch—one of its
prime identification marks.

Unfortunately, the red-cockaded woodpecker will nest in
only two sorts of trees, the loblolly pine and the shortleaf pine.
This by itself poses no problem. But the scarce woodpeckers will
nest in only those trees with "red-heart disease," a plant illness
borne by airborne fungi which attacks old-growth pines. It is
precisely these old red-heart pines, however, which lumber
companies cull from their lands to make room for younger,

healthier trees. The birds are so bound to this type of tree that they are unable to adapt to any other. As more and more old-growth forests have fallen to the bulldozer and the power saw, the woodpecker's numbers have plummeted, placing it finally on the national list of endangered species.

Interestingly, the red-cockaded woodpecker has recently become the center of a bitter controversy. Conservationists, alarmed by the bird's decline, have instituted suits over the management of the national forests in Texas. One would think that national forests would be natural bird sanctuaries, but the red-cockaded woodpecker's decline even there is taken by conservationists (and many others) as proof that the National Forest Service has never taken seriously the Federal Multiple Use Act, which decrees that national forests are to be managed for many purposes, including nature study and bird watching. The red-cockaded woodpecker, through the suit joined on its behalf by the Texas Committee on Natural Resources, the Sierra Club and other groups, has become the Spotted Owl of the American South. It symbolizes old growth forests and their destruction by crude, out-of-control clearcutting policies. Perhaps it will help ensure that some of these forests will continue to exist.

Besides being a haven for rare, scarce, and endangered species, the region serves as a refuge for large numbers of water birds. Wherever one hikes or canoes in the Thicket, he is sure to surprise water birds, foraging along a slough or backwater or perching silently on an outstretched limb. Among these are herons, egrets, roseate spoonbills, cormorants, rails, bitterns, yellowlegs, and wood ibises, America's only species of stork. An interesting recent immigrant is the cattle egret, which has wended its way to the Gulf states from North Africa. How it did this no one is certain. Conceivably it hitched a ride from west Africa to Florida in the turbulence of a tropical storm or hurricane.

To this catalog must be added seven kinds of owl, at least seventeen varieties of hawk, thirty-six sorts of warbler, seventeen kinds of sparrow, and, if one leaves out the ivory-bill, nine of Texas fourteen woodpecker species. The number of warblers is especially striking. The Big Thicket shelters three-fifths of North America's varieties of wood warblers and nearly four-fifths of the warbler species found in Texas. Some, like the Connecticut warbler and Swainson's warbler, are scarce birds.

The list could be greatly expanded to include migrant shore birds, geese, vireos, ducks, flycatchers and many others. It also might have included species like the golden eagle, the Mexican eagle, the sandhill crane, and the caspian tern, which are "occasionals" in the area. But enough has been said. The Thicket is a rich bird sanctuary. It is a national ornithological resource.

From trees, wildflowers and birds to carnivorous creatures is a big jump. But no account of the Big Thicket is complete without a catalog of its meat-eaters. Some carnivores which once existed in the Thicket are extinct; others are merely near extinction. There were reports around the turn of the century of ocelots ("leopard cats") found along the southern margins of the Thicket. It is entirely unlikely that one would find any there now. The nearest known ocelots are dwindling populations hundreds of miles away along the Rio Grande. The writer has argued with biologists who state flatly that it is impossible that the ocelot ever existed anywhere in the Thicket. It is easy to see, however, how the ocelots could have drifted north along the coastal prairies from Mexico. The same holds for Mexican jaguars which settlers once claimed were there too. In fact, both jaguars and ocelots are known to have ranged as far east as Arkansas and Louisiana.

Occasional panthers are seen—and heard—in the Thicket. Auditory panthers in the area are supposed to sound like a screaming woman; visible panthers are almost always supposed to be black; at least, that is the legend. The writer is skeptical indeed about the existence of black panthers. But he concedes that sightings of panther in the region do still occur. What is not clear is whether these are wandering cats, ranging periodically through Southeast Texas, or whether they are permanent residents.

The situation with regard to bear is closely similar. As land once planted in cotton has been turned back into woods and tree farms, and as former tenant farmers have left the land for the greener pastures of town and city, the possibility of bears ranging through East Texas has increased. The possibility of their being shot, however, has remained constant. When one wandered into Livingston, Texas, in the late 1950s it was thought to be the last bear in the Thicket. Sure enough, local citizens shot the animal and barbecued it. According to local legend it weighed around 450 pounds and tasted "gamey."

It appears that, as with the panther, bears sighted in the Thicket—and some have been, recently—are not naturalized there, but are wandering through. Where they may be headed no one knows, but where they come from seems clear. They are from the Atchafalaya (pronounced "Shaflaah") Basin in Louisiana, a broad swampy area that once paralleled the Mississippi River's course to the Gulf. As the bear becomes endangered even in the Atchafalaya, the possibility of its continuing to haunt the back reaches of the Big Thicket decreases.

There are alligators there too—more numerous than bears and panthers and more likely to remain. There are stories of alligators down Big Sandy Creek where it turns into Village Creek before emptying into the Neches River. Occasional swamps in the area may shelter a few, and the number of sightings along the Neches proves that 'gators are managing to hold on there. If poaching could be halted, or even slowed down, the number of alligators would increase significantly. This is no small matter for wilderness ecology. Alligators, by constant digging, manage to keep their water holes from going dry during the summers. They thereby assure a water supply for other game.

Big meat-eaters are spectacular; they are dramatic; and their existence in a habitat attests to its character as a real wilderness. It takes more than a remnant panther or bear, however, to constitute a wilderness ecology. There are also the smaller carnivores—the wildcat and the Texas red wolf, in this case—and the smaller mammals generally. Throughout almost the entire Thicket the wildcat is present, somehow surviving hunters and trappers after its valuable pelt. Far scarcer is the Texas red wolf—a smaller relative of the grey wolf or "lobo" of

Deer in pasture

the western plains. Once found throughout the American South, remaining purebred populations of red wolves are limited to small packs on the upper Texas and Southwest Louisiana coastal prairies. Received wisdom has it that this small wolf survives there, like the Indians before him, by using the prairies during fair weather and heading into the woods when the weather turns. If so the Lower Big Thicket is one of its natural—and last—sanctuaries.

But the word "purebred" has been used here, and its use calls up a word of caution. Originally it was thought that the red wolf was an entirely distinct species which was menaced through interbreeding with coyotes. Geneticists now suspect that it is the other way around, that the red wolf was from the beginning a coyote-timber wolf hybrid, a product of coyote-wolf interbreeding. If so, failure to find perfectly purebred *Canis rufus* would only be proof of its hybrid character. Efforts in North Carolina to produce a reasonably close facsimile of the original red wolf, in any case, make it possible to hope that this carnivore will someday return to its original range.

Hunters have long recognized the Thicket's function as a sanctuary for deer, which still thrive there—or would, if game laws were vigorously enforced. (They have been enforced there on a minimal level since 1964.) Besides deer, there are the other small mammals of the Southern woods: beaver, mink, nutria, muskrat, red and grey fox, flying squirrel, raccoon, opossum, cat squirrel and grey squirrel, and the omnipresent armadillo. The river otter, increasingly scarce in the wild, is found there. The ring-tailed cat, a raccoon-like carnivore of the western deserts, has been reported from Hardin County. Perhaps, like the armadillo, it is expanding its range into green, well-watered country.

No catalog of Thicket mammals would be complete without adding one more creature: the piney woods rooter hog. The "rooter" both is and is not a wild creature. It certainly runs wild in the woods, and of all creatures there—when full grown, and in defense of its young—it is the most dangerous. As the descendent of the Spanish razorback hog and the ordinary barnyard pig it is a hybrid domestic species. Little matter. As Howard Peacock states, all settlers in the woods learned to be wary of it:

[31]

Many boys, in their learning days, got chased up a tree by an old 'tush hog'—the boss hog of a wild pack. Its long tusks, or tushes, were like eight-inch swords, curving from the corners of its mouth; it knew how to maim and even kill with them. Moreover, a typical tush hog had a furious temper.

Though settlers typically gave wild hogs plenty of distance, many lived off them, letting them run in the woods, then rounding them up like cattle for market or for pork chops. The hogs' only natural enemies were bears and panthers.

For a time in the 1940s and 50s the wild hogs themselves were nearly extirpated by hunters. Rooters—which, it is said, can live on a diet of rattlesnakes and pine straw—managed to survive the assault. They are back, sometimes in large numbers. The last time this writer was in the Thicket he came across a herd of rooters consisting of fourteen young and at least three large, fully-developed adults. They bolted into the woods and disappeared. The writer went in the opposite direction.

Finally, there is the matter of snakes. Not everyone wants to hear about them. Daintier sorts rather prefer orchids, ferns, and dogwood trails. Hardier types prefer bears, panthers, and lies about Bigfoot. A brief description of snake life in the Thicket is inescapable, however. All who are repelled by reptiles can skip the next few paragraphs and go on to a section on twilight and palmetto palms.

North America has four species of poisonous snakes, and the Thicket has them all: water moccasins ("cottonmouths"), copperheads, coral snakes and at least four kinds of rattlesnake. With the exception of the cottonmouth, which has an unstable and unpredictable character, you would have to work overtime to be bitten by any one of these. North America's poisonous snakes would, under almost any circumstances, rather run than bite. In the case of the even-tempered and beautiful coral snake, you might practically have to stick your finger in its mouth to be bitten. Children have been known to play with coral snakes for days without getting so much as a scratch. (On the other hand, one hastens to add, coral snakes, like most people, will bite if stepped on or choked, whatever their metaphysics.) The best bet for hiking the Thicket is therefore a set of sturdy boots, and the calm realization that thousands have trekked, fished, and hunted the region for years without getting bitten, or even rattled at.

For every type of poisonous snake in the area there are five or six nonpoisonous species. Some, like the worm snake, the Louisiana pine snake, and the red-bellied snake, are rare. Possibly more rare species will be found. Meanwhile even the commonest—which play their part, too, in the balance of nature—need to be protected. There are more species of snakes in the Big Thicket, biologists tell me, than in any region of comparable size in the United States. With the possible exception of Florida, no *state* contains as many species of snakes as the seven or eight counties of the Thicket. Among the common ones you will find there are: scarlet king snake, indigo snake, blue racer, Girard's water snake, diamond back water snake, Hallowell's water snake, water pilot, spreading adder, blind snake, horn snake, bull snake, sand snake, chicken snake, Texas rat snake, and coach whip. None will win a popularity contest; but all are valuable to their environments and valuable to science.

At best catalogs are efficient; at worst, and at the same time, they become insufferably dull. No preacher ever preached all the Old Testament "begats." One wonders if the Greeks ever sat through Homer's list of ships. Walt Whitman's catalog of sights, smells, sounds at first produces verisimilitude, then an uncontrollable urge to read Ernest Hemingway. The present survey of *flora* and *fauna*, therefore, calls for an apology. In an inventory all items are carefully grouped and numbered. But the real world is much of a muchness. There, plants, birds, mammals, reptiles, weather and water are mixed up together in shifting, subtle, innumerable patterns.

In the remainder of this chapter an effort will be made to analyze the Big Thicket not in terms of enumerated contents, but in terms of topography, plant growth communities, and location. It may be useful at first, however, to describe the Thicket in its "muchness"—through personal acquaintance with its sheer welter, with its shifting, colored, sounding expanse. The following are notes taken on a day's hike down Pine Island Bayou, in the heart of the traditional Thicket. It was made in July—not an ideal hiking month—and, to complicate things, for a time the author was lost. The strong impression was that of being disoriented in a jungle, where nature, not man, held the trumps. The experience, the writer felt, was a valuable one.

The bayou meandered endlessly between low, leaf-matted banks, its water coffee brown and, in the blaze of sunlight, faint green. A fish darted into the green and disappeared; a turtle submerged suddenly from a rotting log. A mile off the road there was woods-silence; insects chirped, frogs chorused, an owl muttered sleepily. No car, no human voice, not even a dog's bark broke the heavy stillness. Mosquitos whined, but strangely, did not bite. A woodpecker drummed on a dead tree, shaking down leaves that rattled on bare branches, clattered onto the forest floor. Wild hogs crashed off, thudding through vines and downed branches and palmetto palms.

From noon to sundown there was no house, or shed, or tilled field. One tire track bisected the bayou and a single pipeline corridor transected it twice. The corridor was empty; its parallel lines disappeared to a point in far-off hazy woods, above grass shimmering in heat. Then woods closed over again, moist and dim. A water moccasin sprawled on a mossed bank, then dropped suddenly into water murk; an egret burst from among tall cypress knees and flew, white against black and green, squawking. An animal, perhaps a fox, fled into the woods so quickly and silently that it was only a moving shadow among palm fronds and vines.

In late afternoon sunlight lengthened. Yellow light streaked palmetto palms, dyeing bayou water and the trunks of big cypress. Owls called to one another through deepening shadows. I should have reached the road, but the bayou shrank, then spread out, taking several courses at once, moving away from itself in erratic curves. I checked a compass and the sunslant, wondering what a night in that place might bring. At noon, distances faded, an odd sameness reigned. Now in the murky

Palmetto Palm

light I could peer back into depth. In the tangle an animal broke a branch, a vine quivered.

It was time to head out of the Thicket, following a game trail, then a path, then faint tire tracks towards the west sun. It took two hours to break out onto the highway; from there it was four miles to a settlement. Up in the pine tops a hawk circled, a wind was blowing. It was the first time I had noticed the wind or sky since noon, when I stepped into the woods. It felt strange to hear a car finally coming down the highway. Everything felt different in the new light of dusk.

Not everyone appreciates the muddy stillness of a looping bayou or the alien green of cypress swamps. Not everyone will enjoy confronting wild hogs on a back road or listening to the muttering of owls in black noon shade. Why do you want that, some will ask? Why is that valuable? Conservationists are used to such questions, and to even more specific ones relating to the diversity, complexity, and biological richness of the Big Thicket. If you cannot tell me in a few words what the Big Thicket is, they ask, how can you expect me to assess its value? And if you can not tell me *where* it begins and where it ends, how can you ask me to "save" it? Such questions are entirely understandable. If all the articles and books written about the Thicket were lain end to end, they would not reach an agreement; no two accounts of it mention exactly the same places; no two maps of it have precisely the same contours. This complexity of opinion presents the conservationist with two clear obligations. He must give a lucid account of what the region is. And he must say it with reasonable precision, otherwise he will be in the position of recommending the creation or expansion of a national park without being able to say where it should be or what it should contain.

If the Big Thicket were a geological feature like a mountain or a canyon there would be no problem. It is an ecological entity, however, and such entities rarely have perfectly precise boundaries. Questions about its mapping simply reflect the kind of thing it is. More broadly, they testify not to its lack of definition but to its extreme variety of soils and plant life and to its lavish biological endowment.

At different times the Big Thicket has been located in different ways. In spite of disputes over details, however, there is a consensus concerning its general location. To pioneers

> ... the name originally applied to the area between the old San Antonio Road and the coastal prairie of South Texas from the Sabine River on the east as far west as the Brazos River. . . . As settlement progressed, it became evident that the impenetrable thickets stopped far short of the Brazos, and the Trinity River came to be considered its western border. (*The Handbook of Texas*, 1952)

The only real exception to this picture is proposed by J. Frank Dobie, who describes the region as extending north to south, 140 miles along the Sabine River (the Texas-Louisiana border) with a greatest width of fifty miles. How Dobie managed this speculation is hard to say. Since no one else has offered such a map, however, we are justified in putting the Thicket back in its traditional place and never again allowing it, as Dobie does, to try to escape into Louisiana.

The *Biological Survey of the East Texas Big Thicket Area* contains a map of the wilderness which closely follows the description given by early settlers. As claimed in the *Biological Survey*, the original Thicket contained all or part of fourteen counties and amounted to 3,350,000 acres—an area (5234 square miles) roughly the size of Connecticut (5009 square miles), or one-half the size of Maryland (10,577 square miles). By the 1930s only a small portion of this area bore the name or appearance of the Thicket.

A much more detailed map of the region was proposed by Professor Claude McLeod, now emeritus at Huntsville's Sam Houston State University. McLeod's map is based on a careful ecological survey and must be taken seriously by anyone who wishes to understand the nature and extent of the Thicket region. According to McLeod the Big Thicket sprawls from the Louisiana border west to near Conroe in Montgomery County. (See map, Figure 1) In contrast to the 1938 biological survey, however, he excludes significant parts of Walker, Trinity, San Augustine and Grimes counties from the Thicket proper. Interestingly, McLeod includes the northeastern tip of Harris County, bringing the region's southwestern reaches almost as near to Houston as its southeastern reaches are to Beaumont.

McLeod's map is based on a convincing definition of the Big Thicket's biological identity. He states:

> As a region it is . . . sufficiently homogeneous in species composition to delineate it from adjacent vegetational types. Likewise the vegetational structure holds in both dominant and understory indicator species through the entire area, thus sustaining both in concept and definition The Big Thicket of East Texas.

Ecologically, McLeod goes on to add,

> . . . the Big Thicket vegetation may be briefly defined as an edaphicmesophytic climax forest type, predominantly a loblolly pine-hardwood association, abounding in a rich understory of both evergreen and deciduous shrubs, a variety of climbing vines, and both annual and perennial herbs.

Even the best definitions can use a little explaining. "Edaphic" refers to soil type. By "mesophytic," he means plant species which exist under conditions of medium rainfall and temperature. By defining the Big Thicket as a "loblolly pine-hardwood association," McLeod means that it must be understood as a region where moisture-loving loblolly pines are found with a specific set of hardwood trees: southern Magnolia, beech, white oak, and in some places swamp chestnut oak. Wherever in Southeast Texas you come across loblolly pines growing among magnolias you almost certainly have found original Big Thicket vegetation.

This unique type of pine-hardwood association, though it distinguishes the Big Thicket from surrounding prairies and piney woods, also stamps it as an extension of Deep-Southern forests generally. The Southern Evergreen Forest sweeps westward from southern Virginia through Mississippi and southeastern Missouri into East Texas. Its southernmost limits are in central Florida; its northeastern limits are in southern Virginia. Its position at the western extreme of this forest explains its admixture of eastern and western plants. Its Gulf exposure guarantees it a subtropical climate and abundant rainfall. Its soil conditions, in turn, help to explain why the Thicket exhibits such an intensification of the evergreen forest just before its disappearance at the borders of the post oaks and blackland prairies to the west. In a nutshell: geographical location explains the Big Thicket's diversity; rich, water-bearing soils explain both its botanical lushness and its pine-magnolia ecology; its dominant species stamp it as an outgrowth of the Deep-Southern forest—the last outgrowth and the most fascinating.

The 1938 biological survey defined the Thicket as a "temperate zone mezophytic jungle." McLeod correctly points out that this definition is misleading as it stands. Large stretches of the original Big Thicket were doubtless deeply shaded forest largely free of vines and tangled undergrowth. These areas must have been open woods, relatively easy to travel, at least by horse—though not by wagons, which would have had a hard time navigating through closely-spaced tree trunks. They were more like the Indians' Big Woods than the pioneers' Big Thicket.

The pioneer's description of the Big Thicket as a *thicket*, however, cannot have been entirely false. It is true that some of the present jungle-like areas there have been produced, as Professor McLeod correctly insists, by felling the "overstory" of big trees. Full sunlight then pierces down to the "understory" of shrubs, vines, and small trees, which then respond with riotous growth. All such "dense" areas, however, could not have been produced in this way. One of the earliest accounts of the Thicket is recorded in the journal of Gideon Lincecum, who came to Texas from Mississippi in the 1830s. Lincecum, an amateur botanist of wide experience, notes crossing big Alabama Creek. On the next day he writes:

This day passed through the thickest woods I ever saw. It perhaps surpasses any country in the world for brush. There are 8 to 10 kinds of green undergrowth, privy, holly, 3 or 4 sorts of bay, wild peach trees, bayberry, etc., and so thick you could not see a man 20 yards for miles. The soil is pretty good and the water the very best. . . .

This was long before anyone had timbered off any part of the region's overstory, even on a modest scale. Lincecum's testimony substantiates the view that extensive parts of the region have always been "thicket" and not open woods. Doubtless both sorts of habitat existed there from the beginning, just as both exist there—though in quite different proportions—today.

The truth here is predictably complex. The Texas Research Foundation's Donovan Correll points out that large areas of the Big Thicket resemble the jungles of Mexico in which he has done field work. The Thicket is not and was never a gigantic jungle. Yet it is one of two places in North America significant parts of which can lay claim to jungle status. The other exists in the southern reaches of the Florida everglades.

This picture of complexity is strengthened by still other factors. The Thicket, McLeod teaches, contains three distinct subregions: The Upper Thicket, the Lower Thicket, and the Stream Thicket. The Upper Thicket is dominated "in its climax form" by a mix of magnolia, loblolly pine, beech, and white oak. (To ecologists "climax form" means the structure attained by a long-standing mature forest.) It is hillier and better drained than the Lower Thicket. More of it is open country, "Big Woods" rather than "Big Thicket." The Lower Thicket is flatter and swampier. It has no beech trees; swamp chestnut oaks take their place. To the east, in Jasper and Newton counties, lies the Stream Thicket. Less continuous and more "gappy" than the Upper and Lower Thickets, it consists of typical Thicket communities along small fast-running streams. Both McLeod's general map and his three subregions have been attacked. Lumbermen protest that the region never reached as far southwest as McLeod insists; conservationists as a rule complain that the

Thicket overflows McLeod's boundaries and takes in adjacent areas.

The writer has examined the terminus point of the Big Thicket southwest of Conroe with Professor McLeod, and has seen there the same loblolly pine-magnolia-beech-swamp oak association that occurs above the Alabama and Coushatta Reservation in Polk County and in Hardin County below Saratoga. There can be no question that the Thicket extends southwest to this point, if it is defined as McLeod defines it.

Some wish to define the Thicket, even more broadly, as an entire region of transition. They would argue that absence of a single "indicator species" does not disqualify an area as part of the Big Thicket. They hold that larger ecological boundaries might emerge if the distribution of other trees and shrubs were studied. Many areas alongside as well as beyond the borders of McLeod's map look suspiciously like Big Thicket, even though "indicator species" may be missing. What sorts of maps could be drawn for palmetto palm, or titi (cyrilla), or longleaf pine or swamp bay magnolia, or other possible species? These all ought to be considered, transition region theorists insist, before the Thicket's boundaries are closed.

Some conservationists accept neither McLeod's views nor theories of a transitional region. Many accept the traditional views of the turn-of-the century trapper and hunter:

> To East Texas sportsmen of 1900 the Big Thicket meant northwestern Hardin and southeastern Polk counties. It was, and by many continues to be, considered to extend eastward. . . . . (*The Handbook of Texas*, 1952)

This particularly dense, wild area along Big and Little Pine Island Bayous—which the writer described above from a hiker's viewpoint—was widely known as a last refuge of bear and panther in the Thicket and particularly good hunting ground for other sorts of game as well. Maps of this subregion (which will be termed here the "Traditional Thicket"), have been published by Francis E. Abernethy and Archer Fullingim. (See map on p. 42.)

BIOLOGICAL SURVEY (1938)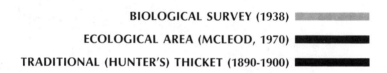

ECOLOGICAL AREA (MCLEOD, 1970)

TRADITIONAL (HUNTER'S) THICKET (1890-1900)

Figure 1. Transposition of three maps of The Big Thicket: Biological Survey, McLeod's Ecological Analysis, and the Traditional Thicket.

[42]

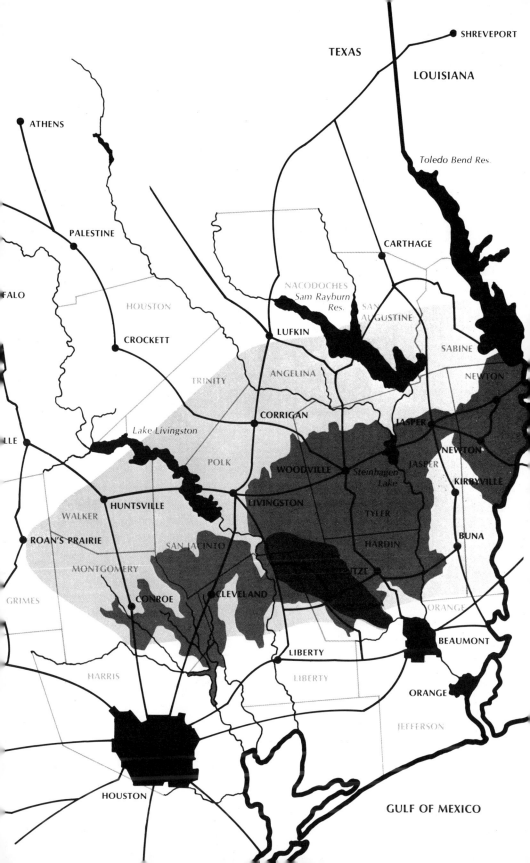

TEXAS

SHREVEPORT

LOUISIANA

ATHENS

Toledo Bend Res.

PALESTINE

CARTHAGE

FALO

HOUSTON

NACODOCHES
Sam Rayburn
Res.

CROCKETT

LUFKIN

SAN
AUGUSTINE

SABINE

TRINITY

ANGELINA

NEWTON

CORRIGAN

Lake Livingston

JASPER

POLK

WOODVILLE

Steinhagen
Lake

JASPER

NEWTON

KIRBYVILLE

LLE

HUNTSVILLE

LIVINGSTON

TYLER

WALKER

BUNA

ROAN'S PRAIRIE

SAN JACINTO

HARDIN

MONTGOMERY

GRIMES

CONROE

CLEVELAND

ITZE

ORANGE

LIBERTY

BEAUMONT

HARRIS

LIBERTY

ORANGE

JEFFERSON

HOUSTON

GULF OF MEXICO

When viewed in terms of Professor McLeod's analysis, the traditional thicket turns out to be a small subregion of the Lower Thicket, which excludes not only most of the Upper and all of the Stream Thicket, but more than half of the Lower Thicket as well. It also excludes reference either to "regions of transition" or to any areas beyond the juncture of Polk, Hardin, and Liberty counties. Many have, like Archer Fullingim, argued long and well for the protection of this subregion with its rich historical associations, dense palmetto thickets, and its still largely undemolished wilderness character. But the traditional Thicket, though it definitely constitutes a distinct subregion, is only that. (See map on p. 43.) It may well be the "heart" of the Big Thicket; but if so, the Big Thicket has legs, arms, veins, arteries as well, stretching far beyond its heart. If justice is to be done to the region, much more than this must be saved.

The problem of where the Thicket boundaries are is closely tied to the question of how it came into existence in the first place. The most detailed attempt to deal with the question of geological origins was made in the 1930s and 40s by H. B. Parks, a leader of the original biological survey. Parks' thesis is straightforward. The present Big Thicket, he says, is a "fossil seabottom." Its low hills are ancient sand dunes, its level stretches are beach margins and former sandflats, its many swamps and bogs are either prehistoric lagoons or ponds, created as dunes trapped retreating waters. Over countless millennia sand, wind, and water labored unknowingly to create it.

This general view of the region's origin is supplemented by Parks with a more detailed analysis. At the end of the Weches Time, he asserts, a new shoreline was created stretching across Texas from just south of Sabinetown to the Nueces River and possibly to the Rio Grande. This shoreline included a bay reaching almost to present-day Huntsville and Nacogdoches and including portions of Louisiana.

> With the coming of the Pleistocene Age . . . the trans-
> gression and regression of the Gulf's water carried in
> sands from the depths of the Gulf and brought back

sands of the Carrizo, Queen City and Sparta Ages, depositing them in this great, flat area.

The region's topography, though this is not obvious to the casual onlooker, thus has all the characteristics of underwater deposits. Present in abundance are the shoals and sandbars marking a receding shoreline. Parks continues: "These sand spits, dunes, and beach lines are now tied down with a wealth of vegetable cover seldom found outside the rain forests of the tropics." Under these conditions the area's soils would necessarily be deposited in irregular patterns, sometimes extending up low valleys miles beyond the original bay or inland sea. This "fingering" of soils provides still another reason, beyond those created by hearsay and legend, why the Big Thicket should prove difficult to map.

Broadly speaking, two contrasting kinds of soil underlie the region. The more recent Lissie Sands were laid down during the Pleistocene. These are now poorly drained and have a relatively high acid content. The Pleistocene soils halt at an abrupt line of hills (the Hockley Scarp), just to the south of Woodville and Livingston. At this point begin the less acid, better drained soils (the Willis Sands) of the Miocene Era. (It is interesting that Professor McLeod draws the boundary between the "Upper" and the "Lower" Big Thicket precisely along the confluence of these two soil types.) An even older band of soils further inland marks the northern boundary of the Big Thicket region. All of the soils of the Thicket have a high capacity to absorb and store water. The Big Thicket ends where its water-bearing soils end, at the edge of the farthest intrusions of the Gulf of Mexico at the time when these soils were laid down.

It would be nice if this image of the Thicket as a fossil sea floor having two distinct soil types expressed the whole truth. In fact, "foreign" soil types are patchworked in among the region's basic soils, with the result that an extremely wide plurality of soil conditions prevails. Some of these interpolated soils are like those along the coastal plains to the south; others are like soils found to the northeast, north and west. Dr. C. L. Lundell of the Texas Research Foundation believes that the Big

Thicket has more types of soils than any area of comparable size in the United States. Hardin County alone, for example, has over 100 soil types.

Parks' theory not only lays claim to the explanation of the Thicket's "sea floor" topology and patchwork of soil types, but to the contrasting origins of its plant species as well. As waters receded in the original inland bay, he speculates, they left behind shoots and seeds of vegetation swept down by ancestors of present-day rivers from the west. Similarly, extraordinary flooding on the Mississippi River during the ice melt of the Pleistocene carried in species from the north, northeast, and east—some from possibly as far away as the Kentucky and Tennessee mountains. Finally, warm Gulf waters deposited plants from the tropics, some of which have thrived in exile. Professor Correll points out, in this regard, that many local wildflowers are Appalachian in origin, and that when their distribution is mapped it becomes clear that they occur in a direct line from Tennessee to the Thicket. Also interesting is the fact that as these species reach the western extreme of their range, they tend to diverge from their relatives to the east. "The variations are often so great," Correll states, "that the plant has to be segregated as a distinct species."

The precise nature of the Big Thicket as a "region of critical speciation" remains to be explained in detail, and is one of the interesting puzzles concerning it. Another interesting conundrum involves the occurrence there of plant growth patterns found in the Appalachian mountains, but not between the Thicket and the Appalachians, which are hundreds of miles to the northeast. Biologists have yet to study the area's micro-ecology in detail; just as its bird and animal life are not fully classified, so its macro-ecology is not yet fully studied.

While the taxonomist classifies living things via their similarities and dissimilarities, the ecologist studies the dependence of organisms both on each other and on their physical environment. Plants and animals exist not as rugged individualists, but in communities. So delicate is the balance of many communities that the elimination of one species may cause the disappearance of several others and force radical changes in the environment. Fortunately the unusual variety of the Thicket has, along with other factors, helped to stabilize and thus protect its ecology. Where one plant or animal has been rooted out, others have often been able to step in and take its place.

Ecologists distinguish eight distinct plant communities in the Big Thicket: upland communities, savannahs, beech-magnolia communities, baygalls, palmetto/bald cypress/hardwood communities, bogs, streambank communities, and floodplain forests. If one adds to this list the various natural prairies found there, the number of plant communities comes to nine. A slightly different analysis is proposed by Geraldine Watson in her *Big Thicket Plant Ecology*. Collapsing baygalls and acid bogs into a single community, she arrives at a grand total of eight: upland pine savannahs, beech-magnolia-loblolly pine communities, palmetto hardwood flats, swamplike communities (acid bogs and baygalls), streambottom hardwood communities, wetland savannahs, prairies, and arid sandland communities.

Interestingly, Watson's analysis adds to basic Thicket ecology an entirely different sort of association, the arid sandland community, quite unlike the others and replete with species from the arid west. There is much to be said for this classification. In what follows, however, the earlier classification proposed in 1967 by the National Park Service will be used. By now no one will be surprised at being told that the existence of two or even more schemes for classifying area plant communities is just one more proof of the area's exuberant botanical variety and its potential for scientific research.

Between these associations there exists nearly every conceivable kind of gradation. The 1967 National Park Study states:

> The forest contains elements common to the Florida
> Everglades, the Okefenokee Swamp, the Appalachian
> region, the piedmont forests, and the large open wood-
> lands of the coastal plains. Some large areas resemble
> tropical jungles in the Mexican states of Tamaulipas
> and Vera Cruz.

Each plant community existing throughout the entire range of the Southern Evergreen Forest can be found in the Big Thicket. It is the only segment of the Southern Evergreen Forest of which this can be said. One would search without success to find such a mingling of species and communities elsewhere on this continent.

Faced with facts like these, conservationists have often brandished phrases like "America's best-equipped ecological laboratory" and "North America's Environmental Ark" to describe the Thicket. Such phrases constitute grand rhetorical flourishes, but they reek of exaggeration, and exaggeration is often considered to be an endemic low-grade infection of most Texans (the author included). Can't environmentalists manage to avoid such exaggerations, and still make their point?

What is surprising, however, is that both these phrases and the claims they express are really not exaggerated. Strange as it may seem, they are understatements. The basis for this claim is provided by Professors Thomas Eisner and Paul Feeny and colleagues, of Cornell University, who have done field work in the Big Thicket and on all of the world's continents. Not only is it unique in North America, they have argued in congressional hearings, but its diversity is also unparalleled in the Earth's Northern Hemisphere. Such diversity could conceivably have occurred elsewhere, they point out. But the occurrence of so many tropical and subtropical species in one place has been prevented elsewhere by such obstacles as the Sahara Desert, the Mediterranean Sea, and the Himalayan Mountain Range.

As already explained, diversity, in addition to being a blessing, can also create quandaries. This is certainly true in the present case. The Big Thicket is no longer a single contiguous wilderness and can no longer be preserved simply by being set aside as one park. Which areas, then, should be "saved"?

As late as 1938 biologists could state that over a million acres of the region remained untouched by plow or axe. A single 400,000 acre tract could in those years be proposed for a national park. By the time the recent Big Thicket conservation movement could begin to generate support, the wilderness was generally agreed to have been reduced to around 350,000 acres and was estimated to be shrinking at fifty acres a day. Faced with these hard facts, a park of 100,000 to 200,000 acres was proposed. Lumber companies responded with plans for a 35,000-acre National Monument which they titled the "String of Pearls."

It is interesting to look at the "String of Pearls" from today's vantage-point. Insufficient though nearly all conservationists agreed the pearls to be, this lumber-company- inspired plan did concede some fundamental factors on which there was general consensus. These were: that certain ecological areas should be set aside and protected, that these areas should contain specimens of the basic habitats of the Thicket, and that they should be large enough to ensure preservation.

Later in this book the struggle to conserve the Big Thicket and the controversies surrounding various proposals for parks and monuments will be described at length. What follows here will be only a bare outline, but an outline very helpful in making evident both the region's diversity and the difficulties diversity creates.

Originally the following nine "pearls" were proposed by the National Park Service:

1.	Beech Creek	6,100	acres
2.	Neches Bottom	3,040	acres
3.	Loblolly	550	acres
4.	Hickory Creek Savannah	220	acres
5.	Beaumont Unit	1,700	acres
6.	Big Thicket Profile	18,180	acres
7.	Little Cypress Creek	860	acres
8.	Tanner Bayou	4,800	acres
9.	Clear Fork Bog	50	acres

Of these, the first five finally ended up being protected, though under conditions quite different than those originally envisioned by the National Park Service. The same is true of a small portion of the Profile area. The Little Cypress Creek and Clear Fork Bog were later clearcut, while the Tanner Bayou section remains today both unprotected and essentially wild.

Beech Creek, as its name proclaims, is primarily a beech forest, with its share of magnolia and loblolly pine. It is therefore a prime example of the beech-loblolly-magnolia association which McLeod identifies as the symbol of the Big Thicket. The Neches Bottom Unit and the Beaumont Unit, though contrasting in certain respects, (the Beaumont Unit fronts on brackish water and is only slightly higher than sea level), are the same sort of swamp-laced hardwood bottomland, containing ancient timber, some of which dates back before earliest settlement. The Hickory Creek Savannah Unit, like Beech Creek, bears its portrait in its name. A grassland partly covered in trees, this area also contains more than its share of wildflowers, including orchids. The Loblolly Unit is a stand of virgin loblolly pine, uncut because of its involvement in litigation, beginning early in the century.

Beginning at the Alabama and Coushatta Reservation on Highway 190, the proposed profile unit would have stretched from there into the Lower Thicket, taking in part of the Traditional Thicket. On the way it would have included parts of three important stream courses: Big Sandy Creek (seven miles), Menard Creek (five miles), and Pine Island Bayou (twelve miles). On the way it would have taken in samples of upland communities, baygalls, bogs, streambank communities, swamps, and palmetto-hardwood habitat.

While not denying the variety and botanical wealth of these "pearls," Big Thicket conservationists were highly critical of the Park Service's proposals. How much is enough, they asked? Can a mere 35,000 acres possibly represent a wilderness that once covered millions of acres? Should the rest of the Big Thicket be sacrificed and only these few pockets of wilderness remain? Not only that, conservationists protested, but the proposed Monument also left out too many ecosystems, too much valuable detail: fern valleys of great beauty, arid sandlands, sphagnum bogs, heron rookeries, tupelo bogs, pre-Civil War log cabins, creeks which (unlike Big Sandy Creek, for example) are canoeable, prairies, oxbow lakes, cypress sloughs. Should not these areas too, they argued, receive protection?

In the face of objections like these, lumber, oil, and real estate interests went on about their business just as before—but with frighteningly greater efficiency. One example of this efficiency was the "soil shredder." These were employed by lumber companies on semicleared land to destroy not only all stumps, vines, grasses and flowers above the ground but also all root networks (or anything else living) reaching to about three feet below the surface. The remains were then planted in rows of slash pines minus hardwoods, flowers, vines, bushes, ferns and the animals and birds that depend on a mixed ecology. ("If there are any birds in there," the writer once heard a biologist quip, "they better carry knapsacks. There's nothing in there for them to eat.")

Soil shredders are extreme examples of the new clearcutting technology. Brush hogs and bulldozers, also commonly employed, achieve very nearly the same results. Conservationists protested bitterly when lumber companies sent workers into the Big Thicket with orders *to girdle every hardwood tree on their lands*. No distinction was made between one ecosystem and another. Company orders included hardwoods in swamps, creekbeds, sloughs, and lowlands of every description where pine trees either could not grow or could grow only badly. What was the point of such policies, environmentalists asked. It could not be simply the desire to produce more pines.

3

Lance Rosier

During the decades when lumber companies bulldozed and cut and stripped, more than a few of those who had fought to defend the wilderness quit, or soured, or even joined the opposition. It was easy to see why. Every time the goal seemed within reach a rumor would be spread, or a fight would break out among the conservationists. Amidst the confusion the image of a green, ancient, inviolable land would slide out of reach.

In the face of these and a hundred other sad aggravations, Lance Rosier never seemed to falter. When others despaired he would walk into the woods and commune with a fern-covered oak or a soaring hawk, and then return to lead someone else— a biologist, a painter, or a reporter, or some brash kid out of college—back into the Thicket. The influence of this quiet gentle man was immense. Scarcely any of those who were involved in the effort to save some portion of the region did not know him, and were not touched by him. He became, almost, the patron saint of Big Thicket conservation. No account of the environmental struggles which involved the region beginning in the 1960s would be complete without a description of his life and his work.

One of those brash kids out of college was the writer of this book, who appeared on Lance's doorstep in Saratoga one day entirely without warning, with a couple dozen questions about the Big Thicket. Like nearly anyone else who appeared, and asked, the writer soon found himself hiking among the palmetto palms and moss-hung hardwoods of the traditional hunter's Thicket, beginning to stagger under the burden of Lance's erudition. For there was scarcely anything that flew, bloomed, walked or crawled within a thirty mile radius of Saratoga that Lance didn't know. "To know," for him, meant not merely the ability to recite a common and a Latin name, but to explain preferred habitat, annual life cycle, and even, where applicable, a medical or industrial use. The writer learned to carry a pad on hikes with Lance, and to fill them with close-cropped notes.

The title "Mr. Big Thicket" was bestowed on him for his persistent labors as a guide, spokesman, and botanical resource. There was an irony in that. Looking at him you would never have bestowed the word "big." His eyes were gentle, distant, and etched with smile lines; frail-looking and wizened, he would not have topped 120 pounds, soaking wet. Yet he could walk anyone, of any age, into the ground. There was beneath that frail, slight exterior a well of stubborn energy. The college kid labored to keep up with him.

There were a lot of things about Lance that were not obvious. It was not that he kept secrets: he just never got around to talking about himself. People could recall that he never got beyond the sixth grade, and that he had begun to learn the Latin names of plants and animals when he worked as a guide for scientists during the biological survey of the 1930s. From the number of books and articles tucked away in nooks and crannies in his small house it was clear that he had learned a lot since then. His house, tucked away behind the Saratoga post office, was in fact a library.

People could also remember that Lance never married, and that when other young adults were playing sports or finding jobs in the oil patch Lance was out wandering the woods, finding colonies of wild orchids and heron rookeries. It does not take a rocket scientist to figure out how much kidding—and how much cruel sarcasm—he had to take because of it. Lance told Louis Hofferbert:

> I was a black sheep. When other boys played baseball, I hunted flowers. When older boys hunted

jobs, I hunted shrubs and plants. Everybody looked down on me. Even my own folks.

As time passed, he was able to put it all into perspective, however. "In those days of course," he would grin, "a man with a rose bush in his yard was considered henpecked."

Local people, who had known him when he would disappear into the woods for days with a pad of paper in one pocket and a cold sweet potato in the other, could never quite believe that he had become a favorite target for newspaper reporters and photographers. "Why," they would puzzle, "he don't do nothin' but prowl those woods lookin' for varmints. Why that's all he ever done. And here these people come clear from Washington just to talk to him." Clearly, it did not make sense. From his shy, weather-beaten face it was impossible to guess Lance's age. It got to be almost a sort of parlor game to try. For more years than anyone knew he had been claiming to be sixty-two.

It was hard to believe he had ever been young. But when he was lying near death in a Beaumont hospital an old country woman came up to a group of Lance's friends and said how much she had loved him: "He was the best dancer. We used to dance all night long at parties when we were young." Lance's friends were astonished. No one had ever known he could dance. Nor did they know, until the woman told them, that he was a fine piano player too.

It even took a while to find out that he had a sense of humor. A one-ring circus was making the rounds in East Texas when its baboon, one of its meager animal collection, died. The creature was unceremoniously dumped in a ditch, as the circus went to its next thrill-packed engagement at a sawmill clearing. When it was found, no one in the Thicket could tell what it was. Clearly this was a case for Lance Rosier, who was immediately fetched from Saratoga. Lance leaned over the back of the pickup and cocked his head. "Well," he drawled, "from the look on its face, and its stooped neck, and the calluses on its britches, I'd say it's a retired East Texas domino player."

Some admiring writers tried to canonize Lance as a sort of latter-day Saint Francis of Assisi. Lance viewed all such efforts as absurd. In one respect, as F. E. "Ab" Abernethy suggests, he acted as a kind of priest, an intermediary not between man and God, but between man and nature. In no way, however, did he think of himself as especially anointed. Nor did he feel called on, as Saint Francis had, to deliver sermons to wolves or sparrows. It is true that he had a green thumb. If he could not grow a bush or a flower in his yard, the odds are very strong that it would not grow anywhere else in the Thicket. Though he never delivered sermons to birds, the writer often saw him pick up a big golden spider it his hand, talk to it, and set it back down on its web without getting bitten. The writer did not try to duplicate this triumph.

The thousands who went on Lance's tours remembered them as unique hybrids of the jeremiad and the botanical lecture. The impression was pleasant, but provocative. In his *Farewell to Texas*, U.S. Supreme Court Justice William O. Douglas buoyantly describes one of these outings:

> The dogwood and the redbud made even cutover land seem gay and joyous. But the rhododendrons and azaleas we saw were the most striking of all. The order of flowering for the shrubs of the Big Thicket is as follows: cross vine, yellow jasmine, hawthorn (of which there are 20 species), azalea and rhododendron, wisteria, dogwood and smoke tree. All but the smoke tree were on display when we hiked Menard Creek. And the showiest were the azaleas that sometimes stood so thick that they looked like a planted hedge. The flower that caught my eye was a huge pink one as large as the orchid one buys at the florist for his lady.

On this trip, Douglas reports, Lance discovered a low blueberry, just starting to bloom, that fruits in the early summer and makes excellent preserves. He also pointed out a tree variety of blueberry that fruits in the fall and is prized by the birds. He found a small, very poisonous shrub. "But it is useful," he added. "The sap is used to make varnish. It is also useful to make animals. Fifteen species of birds and the cottontail rabbit feed on it." A handful of huge old cypress that had escaped the ravages of the lumber industry along Menard Creek stood in splendor in a bog. Justice Douglas stopped to make a boring in a loblolly pine; thirty-two years old, it had a diameter of fourteen inches. "It's now big enough to be commercial," Lance volunteered. A white-eyed vireo sang in a treetop. Somewhere back in the woods a pileated woodpecker hammered a hardwood.

It was just like Lance to know which plants were useful for treating diabetes, for folk medicine, or for making fine lacquers. He was never so happy as when he could show the usefulness of wilderness.

A typical Rosier tour would lead through the hardwood and palmetto country along Pine Island Bayou. He would talk to a group about resurrection ferns, symbiosis, and epiphytes until the massive hulks of dead trees finally roused their curiosity:

"Lance, what killed those big cypresses?"

"Oil wells, up on Batson prairie."

"You mean they struck a gusher up there, and the oil got in the bayou?"

Lance would shake his head.

"No, it was salt water. They let it overflow in here. It killed all the cypress clear downstream twenty miles."

"Didn't they try to stop it?"

"They don't care. I've seen them, when we get a heavy rain; they go out and take the gates out of the overflow ponds. They figure no one will notice it when the bayou's full."

"But they have to build ponds now. I mean, big enough to hold the salt water."

"What's the use of ponds, if you let it all back into the bayou?"

He would then straighten up and talk about the world's tallest cypress that had been found down in the river bottom not long ago, or about the cypress over on Village Creek that biologists had speculated was probably the world's oldest—older even than the ancient cypress of the Everglades. Then he would casually let drop that there was an even bigger cypress back in the sloughs: dead now, killed over a decade ago by oil well overflow. After listening to Lance, the next time you saw an oil well you would have something to think about besides *Giant*.

Sometimes Lance's jeremiads were subtle; sometimes they were blunt. For years he had taken visitors to see a big heron rookery in a swamp along the Trinity River. In 1963 he took a friend there only to find the birds dead: sprayed from the air with insecticides. White herons, blue herons, water turkey were strewn haphazardly. Nests were tangled with rotted flesh and bone. A putrid smell hung in the air.

"Was it a mistake?" people asked.

"No," he would answer, "How could it have been? You couldn't miss the rookery from the air. And it's not right next to any farm."

"But who would do a thing like that?"

"Oh, somebody fighting the park. They want to make it so that there's nothing left. So they sprayed it from an airplane."

The newspapers, for a while, carried stories about the rookery. Then the matter dropped from sight. Soon football season would be starting.

Berton Rouche described a similar outing with Lance and conservationist Ernest Borgman in the *New Yorker*. The trip began with a hike up the famous "ghost road," an abandoned logging spur running due north from Saratoga to the town of Bragg. Once a thriving stop on the Santa Fe railroad, nothing now exists of Bragg but a crumbling old hotel and encroaching forest. The "Ghost" is a phosphorescent light seen on and off at night by local passers-by. According to legend it is the light of a hunter—some say of a Mexican or a black railroad worker—who went to sleep on a spur railroad and had his head cut off by a train. The ghost is of course looking for its lost head by lantern light.

Though the writer did not get to go along with Rouche and Borgman on this particular trek, he did get a chance, later, to talk with Lance about the ghost light. Lance said that he had observed the light at least twice, once for several hours. It had behaved more like some kind of physical entity than a ghost, receding when he approached, returning when he walked away. Like other observers of the light, he finally got tired of watching it and went home.

After many twists and turns Lance led Rouche and Borgman to the high point of the trek: the Witness Tree, a huge three-pronged magnolia at the intersection of Polk, Hardin, and Tyler counties. The world's largest magnolia, it was estimated to be a thousand years old. The path to the tree was a tunnel through jungle.

> It was real Thicket—a forest floor of fallen trees swamped with brush and briar, and understory of holly and dogwood and gum and oak and maple and hawthorn trailing vines and Spanish moss, and a soaring, pillared canopy of beech and magnolia and loblolly pine. There was no sky, no sun, no sense of direction. We climbed over logs and circled sloughs and ducked under hanging branches, and every log and every slough and every branch looked very much like the last. There were no landmarks. There were only the double welts of the old blazes. We picked our way from blaze to blaze—missing a blaze and circling back and finding it and moving on to the next. We walked for a mile and a half.

A clearing then appeared, and Lance pointed to a big grey stump covered with woodpecker holes. This, he explained, was the famous and historic Witness Tree. Rouche's account of his response is as understated as it is powerful:

> "That stump?" I said. It was a very big stump. It was fifty feet high and at least four feet in diameter. But still it was just a stump. "That stump is the Witness Tree?" Borgman was staring at it too. "What happened, Lance?" he said.

"They poisoned it three years ago," Rosier said. "They pumped it full of lead arsenate. I can show you the holes they bored in to put in the poison. I came in with the experts that made the investigation. We found the holes stopped up with little wooden pegs."

"But why?" I said. "Why would anybody do a thing like that?"

"It sounds crazy," Borgman said.

"Yes sir," Rosier said. "But there isn't any mystery about it. They did it for a warning. They were some of the folks that didn't want the National Monument.

The destruction of the Witness Tree made the papers too, just as it was to make the pages of the *New Yorker*. Confronted, the management of one lumber company denied that it had ever heard of the tree.

"That," Lance mused, "was flat-out impossible. They know all the big trees on their land. They keep catalogues of them. They all do."

So far as I know, in the case of the witness tree or any of the other cases of ecological destruction which he observed, Lance never laid the blame on any person or company. When asked, he changed the subject.

The novelist Thomas Wolfe once concluded from hard experience that it is all right to write about a horse thief, but not to give his street address and telephone number. Lance would sometimes give out an address and phone number, Wolfe notwithstanding. In 1970 Lance asked if the writer would drive him down an out of the way, unfamiliar rutted clay road. Miles later he said to stop and look at something interesting. Ahead a hawk soared through calm afternoon. Beside the car loomed a billboard.

"Well hell Lance, wasn't this supposed to be part of the park?"

"Right in the middle of it," he nodded sadly.

"You mean Uncle Sam decided it isn't good enough?"

"Oh, it's plenty good. But they're cutting it up for vacation homes," he grimaced. "The U.S. of A. won't do anything about it."

The billboard (twenty feet long, ten feet high) proclaimed the existence of Hoop 'n Holler Estates. Here weary suburbanites could come, cheek by jowl, for "life in a Real Wilderness." Many had hoped that the announcement of plans for a national preserve would put an end to the needless bulldozing. So much for hope.

"Drive on in," Lance motioned. "Take some snapshots. Take lots."

A hundred yards from the entrance stood an air-conditioned shack, complete with fluttering orange plastic streamers. The roof sign once more proclaimed the joys of life in a Real Wilderness. Behind the shack, roads were cut subdivision-style, through what had been especially set aside as a uniquely rich botanical area. Yaupon, magnolias, and gum trees were piled like matchsticks. Brush heaps three times the height of the car were piled beside the road.

"The promoter who did this is from Livingston. He says he's helping the Thicket by bringing in jobs and people. Last month a man from the Audubon Society came out here and begged him not to wreck these woods. The promoter got on a bulldozer and knocked down some trees just to show him. It's his land, he said, bought and paid for. He even let the Audubon man take a picture of him on the bulldozer. And another thing," he pointed, "the signs here say 'No Hunting.' And they hunt here all the time."

Sure enough, a man carrying a shotgun walked across the road. He disappeared on the other side, under a "No Hunting" sign. Behind him the foundations of a new house rose incongruously.

"If the law was straight they'd be in jail," Lance snapped. "They picked out nine units for the Monument. This one, you can see what they've done to it—cuts the Profile Unit right in two. They timbered in the Beech Creek Unit. And they want to cut the Loblolly Unit. And that's the last big stand of virgin pine in Texas. Here: why don't you take a picture?"

He climbed onto a toppled tree trunk and stared glumly. For half an hour we took pictures, then headed back to Saratoga. On Lance's front porch lay a copy of the *Pineywoods Press* (Promoting Recreational and Industrial Growth in East Texas). Headlines in the six-sheet tabloid proclaimed that this was the very day of the opening of Hoop 'N Holler Estates. I said goodbye to Lance and headed back to Houston's endless sprawl.

Hoop 'N Holler was not the last subdivision to be cut into the Thicket. Ironically, angry conservationists generated publicity on which the real estate promoters, maddeningly, capitalized. The more land they sold, the more they bulldozed what conservationists were trying to save. Lance watched the "protected places" go one by one: heron rookeries, magnolia-studded woods, cypress swamps, the wild places where you could hear only frogs, birds, the thunder of wind in big trees. Now they were developments with plastic flags and slab foundations. And the emblem of the Thicket was the bulldozer, not the ivory-bill.

In those days Saratoga hosted a Big Thicket get-together every spring. It was a time for country fiddlers, beauty pageants, trail rides, well-developed gossip. Lance always looked forward to it. It was a chance to see his friends, to ask about their children, to swap tales. During the 1969 get-together he stepped out onto the steps of the old high school building, when something gave way. Lance found himself on the ground, his left hip broken. He was rushed to a hospital in Beaumont.

For a while he seemed to be mending. He was back in his house in Saratoga, and then out on the street again—walking, but with a cane. He would toss the cane away and get back in the Thicket, he said, and people believed him. But as the weeks passed he weakened, remaining home alone as the leaves made a brown carpet on the lawn and bare limbs scratched the house sidings. He quit talking about throwing away his crutch.

Towards the end of February, 1970, my wife Elizabeth and I dropped in on him, bringing two friends, Roy and Karen Hamric. Frail and tired, he still insisted on showing us the Big Thicket. Since his hip had broken, he explained, he needed to walk a lot. We got into the car and headed down the old Cotten

Lance Rosier in front of the Live Oak Tree planted
by his father (1970)

Road (named for a pioneering Thicket family) running south from Saratoga. It was a grey day with the wind beginning to warm from the south. Several miles down the road we came to a huge old live oak and Lance asked us to stop.

"My grandfather came here before the Civil War. He had six slaves. People thought he was a rich man because of them. The day they came they planted that oak," he pointed to the massive trunk and mossed, soaring branches. "His house stood yonder."

"There, by that hunting shack?"

"Yes. It was a big old house. But it burned."

Lance limped ahead, pointing out species of plants, confirming recent bear sightings, telling how the lumber companies had sprayed herbicides on seven thousand acres along Ghost Road to kill off everything but pine. He leaned over and struck a beer can with his cane.

"Look," he grimaced. "Civilization has been here."

I couldn't bring myself to tell him. A plan had recently been revealed to drain the entire Traditional Thicket for rice farms and cattle: courtesy the Southeast Texas Resource Conservation Development Project, courtesy the U.S. Department of Agriculture. The plan was to bulldoze Pine Island Bayou, turning it into a ditch with nice straight lines and no messy trees, animals, vines, or swamps in the way. Conservationists asked angrily, why not just go ahead and pave it?

Half a mile off the road he stopped at a dead tree whose bark had been chipped off, leaving a hole nearly big enough to drop a shoe box in. Ivory-billed woodpeckers had done it, he explained. Maybe there were a dozen left in the world. If you destroyed the Thicket they would be gone.

The trouble was, people here did as they pleased. There were no game laws; poaching was the rule. The open places were now closed off by hunting leases. They killed so many deer on one lease that they had to import a new herd from the King Ranch in South Texas; and then they killed those. They had killed out most of the frogs and alligators. They electrocuted fish in the water holes with telephone generators, stunning them, picking them out of the water.

"The Gospel of Ecology is slow getting here," Roy said.

"They won't let it across the county line," Lance replied.

He was finally used to the idea of walking with a cane. When he was young he had been hit by a car, and the injury had left one leg shorter than the other. Every day for hours he had struggled up and down steep stairs in his aunt's house until he was exhausted. It took a year, but he finally managed to walk without a limp. Now the limp was here to stay, Lance conceded. But even so, limping or not, this spring he would get back into the deep woods, he said. He asked us to tell people to keep coming to see him.

The winter sun was starting to sink. Lance posed for a picture in front of his grandfather's live oak. His eyes were distant, and, in the fading light, gentle, though he slumped with weariness. That is how his friends would want to remember him, peering off into the Thicket, seeing it as it had been before bulldozers, power saws, asphalt. How, they wondered, had he kept his positive attitude. He had fought year after year, day after day, always losing, always heeded too late. Yet he remained serene, like some piney lake at sunrise.

A month later, March 12, 1970, Lance Rosier died of cancer, in the same hospital in Beaumont where he had gone after his hip broke. He was survived by two sisters and three brothers. And by a covey of newspaper articles proclaiming that Mr. Big Thicket had died.

Lance's room in the hospital in Beaumont had a window which looked out on a courtyard. In the courtyard stood a large elm tree, its limbs still bare grey with winter but beginning to bud, yellow and green. On the last two days of his life monarch butterflies congregated there, on their great annual migration north. There were thousands of them, swarming in the courtyard, clinging to the grey and faint green trees. How beautiful they were, Lance exclaimed. They were the last thing he saw.

Soon after the funeral was done, the last eulogy was read, and people had about gotten used to the idea of Lance not being around any more, one of his brothers went over to Lance's house and dug up the shrubs and cut down the flowers and vines planted so carefully over the years, leaving the house barren and isolated on packed dirt. Corrugated tin sheets were nailed over the windows. What had been a recess amidst deep green shadows now looked like a sharecropper's shack on worn-out delta land. Even when spring came back to that part of the Thicket, few birds sang there. No wild azalea would again burst into bloom near the sagging porch.

4

Conservation and Anticonservation

The goal of creating a national park in the Big Thicket goes back at least as far as 1927. That was when R. E. Jackson of Silsbee held the first meeting of the East Texas Big Thicket Association. A retired railroad conductor, Jackson had become fascinated by the region while working on trains that passed through its vast expanses and listening to the stories of hunters, timber workers, and settlers. For many years he owned a 22,000-acre wilderness lease at the southeast corner of Polk County: the "Tight Eye" country, known for its jungle-like density and lushness. (The name of this area derived first of all from its impenetrable thickets of titi bush [*Cyrilla racemiflora*] and then, by extension, from its thick, overgrown woods.) Jackson turned his "Tight Eye" lease into a game preserve and brought newspapermen, scientists, and conservationists there. Under Jackson's leadership a campaign to create a Big Thicket National Park gradually gained momentum. By the mid-1930s park proposals were developed and prominent figures were beginning to be drawn into the cause.

In 1937 the Texas Academy of Science, basing itself on the first version of Cory and Parks' biological survey, closed its annual convention with a resolution calling for a concerted effort to secure "scientific protection for the Big Thicket." By then several political leaders had allied themselves with the cause. Among these were Governor James Allred, Congressman Martin Dies, and Senator Morris Sheppard. The Beaumont

Chamber of Commerce echoed the statements of the politicians, and articles backing Big Thicket conservation began appearing in large Texas dailies. To read them is to sense how much has changed since then. A *Dallas News* article in 1937 reads:

> A total of 2,350,000 acres of wooded land, some of it overgrown so thickly with trees and brush that one has yet to cut his way through it, lies northwest of Beaumont a few miles. It is upon this veritable paradise for the nature lover, the hunter and other outdoorsmen that two mighty monsters, oil derricks and sawmills, are encroaching rapidly. . . . Officials of the East Texas Big Thicket Association and other organizations are working incessantly to have the entire forest purchased and preserved as a national or state park. Realizing the stupendous task that confronts them, the far-sighted members of the organization have an alternate plan and believe that it will ultimately be worked out. The association would preserve a tract of land of 430,000 acres which is bordered on the west by the Trinity River. This smaller tract, heavily wooded and containing the bigger portion of the palmetto land, which is so thickly overgrown that it is almost impenetrable, is approximately twenty-two miles in length north and south and twenty-one miles east and west.

One attempts without success today to imagine creating a "smaller" park of a mere 430,000 acres. Less than 15,000 people lived in the Thicket then, and less than 1000 of these were outside of its scattered towns and hamlets. There were few roads, and these were largely shell, gravel, or tire track. Vacation subdivisions were not even gleams in a realtor's eye; many oil field pipelines had not been bulldozed; substantial tracts of virgin timber still stood. No wonder a park of over 400,000 acres was a live possibility.

In November, 1938, the National Park Service, at the urging of Senator Morris Sheppard, began a study of the Big Thicket. The investigation, led by wildlife technician W. B. McDougal and acting regional director Herbert Maeir, was completed early in 1939. On the basis of this survey the National Park Service enthusiastically recommended the inclusion of a sizeable portion of the Thicket in the national park system. Senator Sheppard and Congressman Dies began the fight for appropriations. The Big Thicket National Park appeared to be almost a reality.

But it was not to be. The recent creation of national forests in Texas had made it difficult to ask for more federal funds for the Lone Star State. Senator Sheppard's sudden death was also a serious loss. More important than these factors were events taking place in Europe. The February 2, 1939, *Beaumont Enterprise* juxtaposed two telling front page headlines:

ROOSEVELT ENEMY OF PEACE NAZIS CRY. BERLIN PRESS HURLS TIRADE AGAINST PLAN TO AID FRANCE

BIG THICKET DISAPPEARANCE COMING UNLESS AREA MADE INTO A PARK SAYS R. E. JACKSON

Thicket timber, Jackson lamented, was being rapidly cut; in one or two generations there would be little left. He pleaded for help in saving a unique forest that had just received high praise from the National Park Service and the U. S. Biological Survey. But Austria had already lost its independence and Czechoslovakia had vanished. In seven months Hitler would invade Poland. Plans for war multiplied. The Big Thicket was forgotten.

With the end of the Second World War interest in conservation was slow to refocus. Deeply eroded and divided against itself, the East Texas Big Thicket Association now existed as little more than a paper organization. A January 2, 1955, *Houston Post* interview with R. E. Jackson reveals its leader's frustration and weariness:

Residents of Texas are standing idly by while one of the fabulous natural wonderlands in the nation is being destroyed, says R. E. Jackson. Twenty-eight years ago Jackson called a meeting of nature-lovers, scientists and botanists at his camp in the Thicket and the Big Thicket Association of which he has served continuously as president was formed. As president of the association, Jackson says he spent much of his own money making trips to Washington and to Austin where he pleaded with lawmakers to set up legislative measures to preserve the Thicket for posterity. Each time he tried to have something done, he was told both in Washington and Austin that there was no money for such a venture, he says. And now, after twenty-eight years, he feels that the fight of his association is certainly doomed to failure. Roadways have been cut into the heart of the Thicket, timber is being cut and moved out, and wildlife is being ruthlessly destroyed, he says. Oil company crews are making exploration trips through the heart of the forest, and everywhere they go they are cutting down and killing out rare plants and trees.

Jackson added with bitter irony that a group of Houston conservationists had bought land on the fringes of the Thicket and were busy transplanting there trees, shrubs and flowers that were disappearing in the rest of the region. They called themselves the Little Thicket Association.

It would be misleading to leave the impression that the original Big Thicket movement was the work of only one man. Many names could be mentioned: Larry J. Fisher, whose photographs did more than many a speech to show the beauty of the region; Ethel Osborne Hill, who continued to fight for the Thicket well into her nineties; Donald O. Baird, president of the Texas Academy of Science; Henry W. Flagg, president of the Texas Wildlife Federation; Mrs. Bruce Reid; C. B. Marshall; and many others. If the minutes and other records of the East Texas Big Thicket Association still exist, no one has been able to find them. Few newspaper and magazine clippings have been collected from this era. The history of the East Texas Big Thicket Association and its allies remains to be written, though it is a task that needs doing.

If public amnesia is long-lived, it need not last forever. In 1961 two fortunate events revived the memory of the Big Thicket park. The first was the Department of the Interior's West Gulf Coastal Plain Type Study, which recommended that the Big Thicket be studied further as a possible national park. The second was the decision of Texas' Governor, Price Daniel, to make the Big Thicket an issue in his campaign for an unprecedented fourth term. Daniel's Big Thicket proposals were unique: they included the smallest park ever suggested (20,000 acres) and the largest map of the Big Thicket ever drawn. (Critics of the map stated that they were only grateful that it left out Dallas, Houston, and most of San Antonio!) Daniel's interest in the Thicket was serious and longstanding; he and his brother Bill had for many years voiced their concern for its protection. But his proposals were widely received as a purely political gambit, and his defeat in the election was accompanied by a newly aroused resentment at the idea of any park, of any size. Public negation followed public forgetfulness.

Luckily, however, park opponents overreacted. The sudden appearance of a new drive to create a park was accompanied by the equally sudden appearance of fantastic rumors spread by park opponents. Local people were warned that all local schools would be closed; that millions of visitors would come and take over their homes; that their children would be eaten by government-sponsored bears and panthers. The old bogey of economic disaster was dragged out and refurbished. A park would drive out the lumber industry and destroy all jobs; loss of tax revenue from lands taken over by "the feds" would drive small towns into bankruptcy. No one seemed to heed the argument that a park would bring in a new industry (tourism) to complement an old one (timber). That, of course, might undermine the monolithic control of lumber interests in the region.

Such extreme opposition to conservation finally created its counter opposition. The East Texas Big Thicket Association had

died a slow sad death. On November 13, 1964, a new organization, the Big Thicket Association of Texas, was formed in
Saratoga. For all its tenacity, the old association had been
hampered by provincial viewpoints and lack of connections.
The new association was to act with greater sophistication, and
was thus able to draw very effective leaders into its orbit. Its new
president, Dempsie Henley, was well known throughout Southeast Texas and had played a key role in the formulation of Price
Daniel's drive to create a park. Henley knew how to generate
public support, and how to pry publicity out of the media.

The first objective undertaken by the Big Thicket Association was to try to get the state of Texas to take an interest in the
area. This turned out to be an exercise in futility. The Lone Star
State has been—until recently—dominated by interests apa-
thetic towards conservation. Governor Daniel had created a
statewide committee (headed by Henley) to study the Thicket
as a possible park site, but it was not funded and had only a
semiofficial status. Lumber company representatives were included on the committee, but after the first meeting found it
convenient not to attend. They had, in fact, little to fear. When
newly-elected Governor John Connally finally did visit the
region, he came in an Eastex lumber company plane.

The committee report was duly presented by Dempsie
Henley to Governor Connally on March 24, 1965, to the ap-
plause of several busloads of conservationists who had come to
Austin for the occasion. The governor emitted a couple of verbal
flourishes for the occasion and then forgot about all six recommendations. That was a pity; all six were interesting. First, an
additional 2000 acres—managed as an integral part of the
park—was to be added to the Alabama and Coushatta reservation. Next, a 200-acre camping area was to be created adjacent
to the reservation. A Big Thicket State Forest of 10,000 acres
was to be established south of the camping area, with hiking
trails, riding paths, and swimming facilities. Far south of the
reservation, in the old bear hunter's traditional Thicket, a
15,000-acre wildlife and wilderness area was to be staked out.
This area, south of Saratoga, was to be restocked with animals
once plentiful in the region: bear, panther, turkey, and deer.

Moose, buffalo, English boar and javelina were to be thrown in just for fun. (Actually, the javelina or peccary, the small wild pig of south Texas, was reported in the early days as having ranged through the Lower Thicket.) Fifth, a headquarters for this area was to be set up in Saratoga. Finally, areas surrounding these five features were to be subject to joint state-private control (with a tax break for private landowners) to ensure sustained game and lumber production.

It was not the first good idea to drown in the murky backwaters of Texas politics; nor was it the last. The governor and the legislature remained indifferent. Lumber interests went their way in perfect bliss, thinking the whole thing would be forgotten.

The powers-that-be, however, reckoned without the intervention of a new force: the federal government, in the person of Senator Ralph Webster Yarborough. Raised on the Neches River not far north of the Big Thicket, the senator had long been fascinated with the colorful area and the possibility of its conservation. By far the most effective conservationist in Texas history, he was to be instrumental in creating both the Padre Island National Seashore and the Guadalupe Mountains National Park. It was only a matter of time before his long-time interest in the Thicket would flower in action.

Yarborough's Thicket tour in October, 1965, is fully reported by Dempsie Henley in his *The Big Thicket Story*. The tour included Clarence Cottam of the Welder Wildlife Foundation; Jim Bowmer of the Texas Explorers Club; Bill Bowen, superintendent of the Padre Island National Seashore; Dempsie Henley and Lance Rosier of the Big Thicket Association. These convinced the senator—assuming that he really needed convincing—of the region's unique richness and value. The result was Senate Bill No. 3929 to create a Big Thicket National Park.

There are many twists, turns, and confusions between the introduction of legislation and its passage into law—assuming it ever passes. Yarborough's bill was read twice on October 20, 1966, and referred to the Committee on Interior and Insular Affairs, where it rested in quiet splendor for nearly five years:

Be it enacted by the Senate and House of Representatives of the United States of America in Congress assembled, that, in order to preserve in public ownership an area in the State of Texas possessing outstanding botanical and zoological values together with scenic and other natural values of great significance, the Secretary of the Interior shall establish the Big Thicket National Park, consisting of land and interests in land not in excess of seventy-five thousand acres in Hardin, Liberty, San Jacinto, Polk and Tyler Counties, Texas.

Sec. 2. (a) To establish the Big Thicket National Park, the Secretary of the Interior may acquire land or interests therein by donation, purchase with donated or appropriated funds, exchange, or in such other manner as he deems it in the public interest. Wherever feasible, land shall be acquired by transfer from other Federal agencies.

Any property, or interest therein, owned by the State of Texas or political subdivision thereof may be acquired only with the concurrence of such owner.

(b) In order to facilitate the acquisition of privately owned lands in the park by exchange and avoid the payment of severance costs, the Secretary of the Interior may acquire land which lies adjacent to or in the vicinity of the park. Land so acquired outside the park boundary may be exchanged by the secretary on an equal-value basis, subject to such terms, conditions and reservations as he may deem necessary, for privately owned land located within the park. The Secretary may accept cash from or pay cash to the grantor in such exchange in order to equalize the values of the properties exchanged.

Sec. 3. When title to all privately owned land within the boundary of the park, other than such outstanding interests, rights, and easements as the Secretary determines are not objectionable, is vested in the United States, notice of the establishment of the Big Thicket National Park shall be published in the Federal Register. Thereafter, the Secretary may continue to acquire the remaining land and interests in land within the boundaries of the park.

Sec. 4. The Big Thicket National Park shall be administered by the Secretary of the Interior in accordance with the provisions of the Act of August 25, 1916 (39 Stat. 535; 16 U.S.C. 1-4), as amended and supplemented.

Sec. 5. There are hereby authorized to be appropriated such funds as are necessary to accomplish the purpose of this Act.

There is more to creating a national park, unfortunately, than simply issuing a proclamation. Landowners must be paid for increasingly hard-to-find land. In some cases they prefer to trade their acreage for similar acreage found elsewhere. In the Big Thicket, moreover, overlapping oil, timber, and hunting leases combine with ill-surveyed boundaries and titles dating back to Spanish land grants to make land purchase a knotty problem. Last and by no means least, after passage of the original bill a new one may have to be passed, a "money bill" authorizing appropriations. No wonder there are so many Byzantine twists and turns between the reading of a bill and the reality it attempts to create.

In November, 1965, the National Park Service had made a preliminary survey of the Big Thicket and arrived at favorable conclusions. A year later, as Yarborough was preparing his bill, the Park Service made a second reconnaissance. This time the study was sufficiently thorough to permit detailed recommendations. Following McLeod, an upper and lower Thicket were mapped and "specimen areas" selected for protection. This was the String of Pearls discussed in the previous chapter: 35,000 acres of separate tracts connected (hopefully) with scenic roadways. The lumber companies—the only interests involved in its formulation—were reasonably pleased with it.

As was also discussed in the last chapter, conservationists didn't exactly fall all over themselves praising the proposal. To the objections stated previously the conservationists added several others. What is the use of preserving isolated patches of wilderness if in ten or twenty years they are to be encased in a motley web of red flag subdivisions, filling stations and Dairy Queens? In time these units would lose the very values for which they were created.

They also objected to the minuscule acreage of the units. One goal of a national park—not the only one but an essential one—is to provide the "wilderness experience." That, however, requires distance, a broad expanse of wilderness. Since one component of the String of Pearls was to be a Scenic Highway running down the entire length of the Profile Unit, there were some who doubted that a world-lost sense of wilderness could be found there.

Meanwhile lumber interests moved quickly to embrace— and advertise—the String of Pearls, both in *Stewards of the Land* (a glossy pamphlet distributed free to the unwary) and a powerful, well-financed public relations campaign. A significant part of that campaign included sending PR men to service and garden clubs. These were persuaded to pass resolutions backing the 35,000-acre National Monument on the assumption that this would be backing Senator Yarborough's stand.

If conservationists were critical of the new plan they could also take some consolation from it. For decades lumber companies had said that none of the Thicket was worth saving. Now they had publicly admitted that at least some segments of it were of special value. Their sense of consolation was to be short-lived. Word soon came that the Cypress Creek Unit and part of the Beech Creek Unit—as mentioned in the last chapter—had been clearcut, and their stands of virgin beech and magnolia lost forever. Equally dispiriting, lumber company cutting schedules began to accelerate rapidly. Magnolias, especially, were being mowed down. Professor McLeod had pointed out that these trees are a symbol of the Thicket; now, suddenly, the slow-growing trees were falling by the hundreds. Why was that? At the going rate, a century-old magnolia was worth little—less

Bulldozing a clearcut

than five dollars in railroad ties, to be exact. On his Big Thicket tour, William O. Douglas pointed out that magnolias were being cut by timber companies not only on their own lands but on publicly-owned highway right of ways. Was there no way, he asked, to stop this plunder? None, came the reply. No public figure would dare enforce right-of-way laws in counties where lumber companies control the economic and political machinery.

When questioned by *Wall Street Journal* reporter Dennis Farney, lumber company executives replied that increased cutting schedules were nothing but a response to increased demand for lumber. They pointed out that cutting in the proposed units had been done by local landowners which the large companies could not control. Not long after the publication of Farney's article, moreover, the resplendent Hoop 'N Holler Estates were carved into the center of the Profile unit. At the same time cutting began near Saratoga, in the lower Profile unit. Towering cypress were felled into Pine Island Bayou and their stumps and branches left to rot. How generous it was of the lumber companies, conservationists exclaimed, to sanctify a String of Pearls for an inadequate national monument—especially since they were willing to let the pearls be cut down, one by one.

A reaction, however, finally set in. The cries of conservationists, the efforts of the Big Thicket Association, the potential for endless bad publicity finally moved the lumber interests to declare a moratorium on cutting in proposed monument units. The moratorium began officially in July, 1967. To the credit of lumber companies, the moratorium was never violated. One lumberman, Arthur Temple, Jr., complied with the moratorium by closing a lumber mill dependent on hardwood timber both in and around the Neches Bottom Unit.

Though such acts were admirable, from another point of view the cutting moratorium was a Pyrrhic victory. Throughout the Thicket the new clearcutting technology did more than cut out hardwoods. Bulldozers began to make their appearance by the dozens as hundreds, then thousands of acres were scraped bare after timbering. The result was no longer a mixed pine-hardwood forest with its incredibly varied understory of shrubs, small trees and vines, comprising a complex web of "ecological niches" for insect, bird and animal life. Instead, from horizon to horizon and with no mercy for ponds, swamps, or creekbeds, there were nothing but endless geometrical lines of pines spaced out like corn stalks: biological deserts where transient birds and animals "had better carry a knapsack."

Local folk, whether for or against the monument, united in telling conservationists such stories. What was going on was an attempt by lumber companies to render vast land areas unfit for inclusion in any park: small or large, federal or state. They may well have been wrong in their surmise. But the results were the same as if they had been right.

In the creation of a national park, much depends on the congressman within whose district the park lies. The Big Thicket lay largely in the district of John Dowdy, who would probably be described today as a "boll weevil" conservative. Widely known as a lumber company man, Dowdy had rebuffed any and all overtures from conservationists. Back around 1964 a local lumber executive had earned great fame for himself by snapping to a reporter: "The Big Thicket? Why, the way we're going, in ten years there won't be any Big Thicket." As quoted by Edwin Shrake in *Harper's*, Dowdy claimed that the Big Thicket was merely a "stinking mosquito-infested swamp": "I don't see how anything can be done about a park, no matter what the Sahara Club wants." A congressman who doesn't know, or want to know, the difference between the Sierra Club and the Sahara Club is not exactly an ideal conservationist.

Shrake's lament for East Texas is felt by many. The region is trapped, he sees, between a pioneer legacy which it fights to retain, and an industrial establishment which will destroy it.

Not far from what is now Hoop 'N Holler Estates, weekend cottages for people fleeing Houston and Beaumont, the Indians used to bathe in hot mineral springs and drink crude oil as medicine. The springs are dried up now, panthers are seldom seen, bears wander in confusion as far north as Lufkin, where they are shot trying to escape, and the oil of the Indians has been drilled in dozens of pools that bred boomtowns and formed such giants as Texaco. Senator Ralph Yarborough, a Texas Democrat, is trying to save a piece of the Big Thicket as a national park, but it is perhaps a vain hope. As much as they may feel blood kin to the woods and streams that have nourished them for generations, most of the people who live in the Big Thicket, and in the rest of East Texas, depend for their livelihood on the industries that are destroying them, and so they vote for candidates chosen by big companies.

Shrake's point is embodied in an exchange between himself and a filling station attendant. Complaining about noxious fumes from a nearby paper mill, Shrake complained: "If I lived in this town I'd burn that factory down." "If you lived in this town you'd work in that factory," came the reply.

In 1968, however, to the amazement of just about everyone, Congressman Dowdy introduced a 35,000 to 48,000-acre bill to create a Big Thicket National Monument. By then Senator Yarborough had upped his own proposal to 100,000 acres and national conservationist groups were talking still larger figures. Dowdy's bill was widely felt to be a shrewd tactical move by lumber interests to forestall a still larger park. It is impossible to know whether Dowdy would have persisted with his bill. By the time the next election rolled around he was under indictment for bribery. Though Dowdy's wife ran for his seat in his absence, she was defeated. A young state senator, Charles Wilson, was elected in her place.

The years between in 1967 and 1970 thus turned out to be a kind of stalemate. Texas conservationists, blocked in Congress, struggled to bring the media and the national conservationist organizations around to their way of thinking. Lumber companies responded to conservationist pleas with a public relations campaign of their own. Forced to bide his time, Senator Yarborough fought for funding to turn Guadalupe Mountains National Park and the Padre Island National Seashore into palpable, as opposed to paper, realities.

In retrospect it is clear that no one event broke the stalemate of the late 1960s. Several successive events were required for that. If one event could be pointed to that clearly nudged things into motion and announced that something—at least *something*—was going to be done about the Thicket, it was the United States Senate hearing in Beaumont on May 12, 1970. Although this was to be only the first of many, many hearings and announced little that was new in the positions of lumber interests or conservationists, it *was* a public announcement, reaching all the papers and all the TV stations, that the gummy wheels of Congress were indeed starting to turn, that prominent figures were willing to stake their names on the turning, and that support for a Big Thicket park had finally reached a "critical mass." This Senate hearing, then, was symbolic. It was a catalyst.

Senator Yarborough's testimony, the hearing's keynote address, began with personal reminiscences of his youth in East Texas, but moved quickly to deal with basic economic factors.

> In a recent study sponsored by the National Park Service, conducted by Dr. Ernest S. Swanson, *Travel and the National Parks: An Economic Study* (1969), these conclusions were reached: "The computations made show that national parks contribute as much as $6.4 billion to the sales of a multitude of firms throughout the nation. From this amount, personal income of $4,762,530,000 is generated. . . . Travel to the National Park System resulted in $952 million in taxes for the Federal Government in 1967.

Besides these direct effects, the Senator urged, national parks have indirect effects that are equally important. These include spending on local activities which are not directly linked to the natural beauty of a region. The influx of visitors to national parks has, to take only one example, sparked the creation of specialized provisions for hunting, fishing, boating, swimming, picnicking, and sightseeing on local Indian reservations. Economists estimate that in Colorado alone 1.2 billion dollars are generated from hunting and fishing. Far from being a liability, the National Park Service, with around $102 million annual appropriations, contributes forty-five times this figure back to the American people as increased income—more than fifty-five times when the increased income is stated in terms of gross national product.

Yarborough considered that the advantages of a national park in East Texas, which benefitted little from the economic boom the rest of the state experienced after the end of World War II, had not been fully analyzed:

> Rather than injuring the economy of the area . . . it is clear that . . . a national park would give it a much needed boost, and would help in the development of

a broader and stronger economic base rather than one founded primarily on lumbering.

The proposed park, moreover, would involve the investment of only 3.3 percent of the acreage of the affected counties.

Senator Yarborough's statement, though it covered ground little understood by the general public, stressed factors that conservationists had been trying to explain for years. The testimony of the president of Louisiana's Sierra Club, John W. Fultrell, by contrast, came as a surprise to nearly everyone. The once rural state of Louisiana, he explained, would by 1980 have a population of four million, packed into a ten-mile wide strip along the coast. Louisiana's hardwoods, meanwhile, were disappearing at the rate of 111,000 acres per year. Should their destruction continue at that rate—and what was there to stop it?—by 1990 there would no longer be hardwoods in Louisiana. Since conservation is absolutely at the bottom of Louisiana's list of priorities, there was little hope of saving even small tracts of hardwoods there. Amazing, bizarre, unlikely as it seemed, Fultrell concluded, if the people of Louisiana were to have access to hardwood forests, they must do so through the Big Thicket of Texas.

Not all the protesting was to be done by conservationists. Representing the Texas Forestry Association, Ollie R. Crawford pointed out that the National Park Service, three years previously, had proposed a 35,000-acre national monument. Not only had the Texas Forestry Association endorsed the recommendation, he said, but its lumber executives had literally "walked the land" to point out choice ecological areas to Park Service personnel. The association had subsequently backed a voluntary moritorium on timber cutting in the proposed monument units. Far from cutting down the Thicket, he protested, lumber companies had ". . . regrown the Big Thicket that was practically destroyed in the past." The Texas Forestry Association, Crawford concluded, had never fought the park.

If Crawford had stressed the lumber companies' quite understandable desire to protect their "land base," and had hammered home large recent acreage losses through dams, lakes, enlarged highways and urban sprawl—well over 100,000 acres in recent years—his claims would have been understandable. But who could believe that the Forestry Association had never fought the park?

Ralph Yarborough leaned over the rostrum and stared pointedly: "Isn't it true that the Texas Forestry Association has had two men traveling full-time around Texas getting endorsements for the 35,000-acre National Monument?"

Crawford's denial provoked a second question: "Isn't it true that, just before this hearing, the Texas Forestry Association brought in reporters from all over the state on a chartered plane to give them propaganda against the park?"

Crawford replied that this was just their way of "telling one's own story." But he did not look up as he said it.

It was not until late in the day that a rumor surfaced. Village Creek was to be stripped of timber and dammed to provide recreational facilities. That segment of the Thicket would then lie under twenty feet of water, safe from conservationists and students of ecology. Texas—which already had more lakes than Minnesota—seemed hardly in need of a new lake.

Testimony continued from early morning through mid-afternoon, when the senators embarked on a helicopter tour. Unfortunately, the choppers lost their way en route to the Indian reservation and strayed over farm and industrial areas. "I began to wonder," quipped Dempsie Henley, "if the Texas Forestry Association hadn't arranged for the helicopters." Apparently, however, the senators, press, and park service leaders were impressed. Senator Allan Bible, who presided, stated that this was the best national park hearing he had ever seen.

Senator Yarborough was supposed to be in the Texas Hill Country on the following day for a ceremony dedicating Lyndon Johnson's birthplace. But he had heard a rumor to the effect that the hearings were a mere show, and that there would never be a national park. To answer the rumor he appeared unexpectedly, full of enthusiasm, at the annual Saratoga Big Thicket trail ride and get-together. "They say the Thicket hearings don't mean anything," he proclaimed to a crowd of two hundred

Thicket supporters. "That's just hogwash. It might not be tomorrow, and it might not be a year, but there is going to be a Big Thicket National Park. There will be more rumors that if there is a park they will close your schools and there will be no jobs. That's hogwash, too. The schools will stay open. And you'll hear rumors that the government will come in and throw people off their land if there's a national park. That's hogwash. And the people starting those rumors know it's hogwash. National parks create jobs. Pulp timber gives you a crop every ten years; tourists give you a crop twelve months of the year."

5

Getting There

"It might not be tomorrow and it might not be a year, but there is going to be a Big Thicket National Park." In the years to come, conservationists were to cling to Ralph Yarborough's words all the more tightly as hopes for a park waxed and waned, materialized and then vanished again, like the ghost light out on Bragg Road.

When I reflect on this most frustrating of processes, I am reminded of an old, homely story. In the riverbottom where my father was raised, and where I spent a great deal of time as a boy, there was a sandy tiretrack road that local people claimed "was laid out by a drunk, on a blind mule, in a sandstorm, at midnight." It looped and relooped through bottomland tangle, rejoining itself, departing in unknown directions, rejoining itself again. On that road one could make the most determined effort to get to the riverbank, only to come out at the place one began, headed in the opposite direction.

Conservationists—indeed, all those involved in the debate over the preserve—were to feel more than once that they had entered a similar bottomland maze. During his final days in office (having been defeated in the Democratic primary by Lloyd Bentsen) Ralph Yarborough was finally able to get the Senate to pass his Big Thicket National Park Bill. At the last minute, however, an amendment was tacked on to limit park size to "100,000 acres or less," in spite of the senator's efforts to secure a larger acreage. A similar bill, sponsored by Congressman Bob Eckhardt, could not be brought before the house for passage. The chairman of the relevant committee had taken the occasion to go touring in Southeast Asia. The Big Thicket National Park had been headed off. The process had to start again in the next session of Congress.

In the past the Big Thicket had suffered in the state capital and in Congress from a kind of legislative poverty. Now it was to suffer from a surplus of National Park Bills. Actually, the legislative eruption began before the passage of Senator Yarborough's bill. In 1966 and 1967 he had introduced virtually the same bill, followed in June, 1967, by a similar bill introduced in the House by Congressman James C. Wright of Fort Worth. In January, 1969, Yarborough again filed a bill for a park of "not less than 100,000 acres." He was opposed in October by Congressmen John Dowdy and Earl Cabell, who introduced H.R.14391, the lumber interests' "string of pearls" bill, mandating a 35,000-acre national monument. But this was not the end. In July, 1970, a young Houston congressman, George W. Bush, introduced H.R.18498 to create a Big Thicket National Park of 150,000 acres: an objective he was to stress strongly in his unsuccessful Senate race against Lloyd Bentsen. Congressman Bush and his wife had toured the Thicket earlier in the year, and his bill contained most of the areas presently in, and scheduled for inclusion in, the Big Thicket National Preserve. Bush's bill—conceded by most conservationists to be one of the best introduced during the long struggle to create a park—was soon joined by that of Bob Eckhardt, whose H.R.18527 proposed a park of "not more than 185,000 acres." Called the "wheel of green," Eckhardt's bill contained much that was in George Bush's bill plus additional greenbelts and stream corridors.

On January 25, 1971, newly elected Senator Lloyd Bentsen (D.-Tex.) allayed conservationist fears in taking over Senator Yarborough's place by introducing S.118 to create a Big Thicket National Park of 100,000 acres. It was the first bill he was to introduce as a senator. Not to be outdone, Senator John Tower (R.-Tex.), two days later introduced S.378 to create an 81,472-acre park plus 100,000 acres of recreational lands in adjacent national forests. Essentially this park consisted of the lumbermen's "profile unit" plus the "Saratoga Triangle": an area along Little Pine Island Bayou bounded at each vertex by Saratoga, Sour Lake, and Kountze.

If conservationists were pleased—though puzzled—by this legislative largess, they were to discover that it was just the beginning. Early in February, 1971, the New York Times published an editorial backing a Big Thicket National Park of 191,000 acres. It seemed as if the *Times* turned a magic spigot. On February 4, Congressman Eckhardt reintroduced his bill H.R.3618, this time raising the ante to 191,000 acres. On the

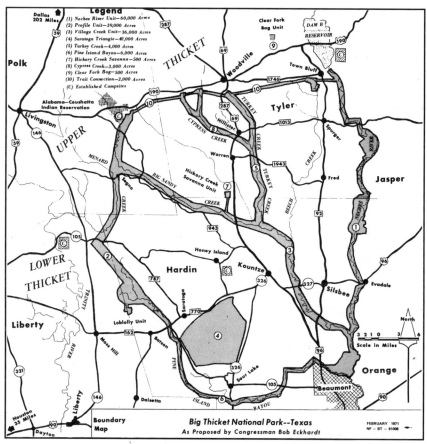

Bob Eckhardt's Reserve Bill

same day Congressman Jake Pickle (D.-Tex.) introduced a 100,000-acre bill (H.R.3575). On February 10, Congressman Jack Brooks (D.-Tex.) introduced H.R.4201 to create a park of 100,000 acres. On March 2, Congressman Earl Cabell (R.-Tex.) introduced H.R.5378 to create a National Monument of "not less than" 35,000 acres: the old "string of pearls" bill, slightly amended. A little over three weeks later Congressman Wright Patman (D.-Tex.) introduced H.R.6556 to create a 100,000 acre park.

Now there were two bills in the Senate and six in the House. It was hard to imagine there could be more, but between 1966 and 1974 there would be twenty-eight separate pieces of Big Thicket legislation!

There were many causes for this welter. One was the early disarray among the conservationists. What was the Big Thicket? Where was it? What/where, exactly, did the conservationists want to conserve? Different factions were liable to give different answers to these questions. (After all, was one dealing with a biological reality or a region defined by legend and folklore? And, if this puzzle was solved, did one stress the Saratoga Triangle for inclusion or Beech Creek, or Jack Gore Baygall?)

These problems were solved, at least on a practical level, by the creation, in December 1968, of the Big Thicket Coordinating Committee, whose task was to achieve consensus among conservationists and to present a united front to both the media and political leaders. On a more profound level they became resolved, or at least were made resolvable, through the work of biologists like Claude McLeod and Geraldine Watson, who made a biological definition of the "Thicket" possible.

Even so, early disagreements among conservationists continued to haunt their later efforts much as the early legends of ghost lights, outlaws, escaped slaves and confederate deserters continued to haunt the Big Thicket. It is no wonder that, presented with a phalanx of problems, along with the adamant opposition of most lumber interests, the National Park Service and its owner and proprietor, the Department of the Interior, continued to hesitate and to postpone public proclamations. When proclamations finally emerged, they expressed contrast-

Tupelo Swamp

ing views. The Thicket was first proposed as a national park, then as a national monument, then as a national recreational area, then as a national cultural park. It took ten years for an acceptable designation to emerge: a new designation, involving new notions of what conservation ought to do.

Nineteenth-century parks were created primarily for their scenery, as if Yellowstone or the California redwoods were precious works of art, to be admired like the Mona Lisa or a fine painting by Turner or Constable. Or, if they were not treated as works of art, then they were at least conceived of as awe-inspiring stage settings among whose grandeur American gentry could meditate—and posture. A place like the Big Thicket, however, even if it possesses natural beauty, does not exhibit the towering magnificence of the Rockies. Its charm is more in the small and the near than in the vast and the remote. Moreover, national parks at this time (most of them in the West), consisted of vast contiguous blocks of land—easier to fence off and protect than river corridors or "strings of pearls." It is no wonder that the Park Service and Interior Department spoke in defense of the Thicket only when absolutely required to. In October, 1971, Secretary of the Interior Rogers C. B. Morton made a statement of support for federal preservation of the Big Thicket. It was a welcome gesture, long overdue. But Morton made no definite proposals. He proposed "in general"— a safe thing to do.

Pleased with Morton's support but frustrated by his lack of specificity, conservationists meanwhile embraced Bob Eckhardt's 191,000 acre proposal, with its definite units and many corridors. To them, the "Wheel of Green" was (to mix metaphors) a beacon of light in a dark political muddle. True, the "Wheel" scarcely measured up to the 400,000-acre park proposed in the 1940s. But it saved significant parts of what conservationists thought should be saved and it connected these together with corridors. It was, they believed, a union of large pearls with plenty of string. If lumber interests eyed it with deepest foreboding, conservationists regarded it as nearly perfect: indeed, as almost too good to be true.

Which it was. Hoping to strengthen the ecologists' case by depicting specific areas for preservation and by claiming a size for the proposed park that made it appear imposing, the congressman soon found himself stymied wherever he turned. Senate subcommittee staff informed him that the Senate would not move until the House passed a Big Thicket bill. Members of the Texas House delegation refused to back his 191,000-acre wheel of green. Some members of the delegation, however, hinted that they might support a 100,000-acre bill. Frustrated at every point, Eckhardt began work on a bill for 100,000 acres: a move which shocked most conservationists and sent a wave of protest through the Big Thicket Coordinating Committee.

Not only were most conservationists upset by the cutback in acreage; they were angry over Eckhardt's abandonment of the Saratoga Triangle, an area which had been known since the turn of the century as the Traditional Big Thicket, and which had been promoted for over half a century by Lance Rosier, the famous Thicket guide. In the words of James Cozine:

> Finally, Keith Osmore, Eckhardt's legislative assistant, met with the coordinating Committee in October, 1971, to hammer out a proposal which would satisfy the preservationists and also meet the 100,000 acre figure. The Coordinating Committee almost dissolved in disputes over the compromise. Each wilderness group on the committee had its own special area that it hoped to preserve. Consequently, each organization fought to retain its pet region in the bill. Eventually, after four tumultuous sessions, the Committee drew up a new 100,000 acre plan to present to Eckhardt.

To call these meetings tumultuous is barely to express their intensity and their friction. The four sessions took up major parts of four long weekends. In the end, conservationists reached consensus as much through exhaustion as through necessity.

Eckhardt's efforts to achieve consensus among conservationists were more successful than his efforts with the Texas
delegation. On December 2, 1971, he and Congressman Jack
Brooks of Beaumont compromised, co-sponsoring a 100,000-
acre bill (H.R.12034) which specified no particular areas to be
saved. The bill was signed by nine other Texas congressmen and
was accompanied by an identical piece of legislation introduced
in the Senate by Lloyd Bentsen. Over Eckhardt's objections the
Texas delegation had produced a faceless bill, proposing acreage
that might be fenced off anywhere at all.

In protest Eckhardt three days later introduced his own
100,000-acre bill mapping specific areas to be saved—essentially those agreed to by the Coordinating Committee. This bill
was cosigned by Congressmen Jim Wright and John Young.
Then, as the disputes dragged on, Congress took the occasion
to adjourn. Legislative machinery ground to a halt. Bulldozing
and clearcutting, unfortunately, did not.

In February, 1972, Congressman R. Roe (D.- New Jersey),
introduced H.R.13038 to create a 191,000-acre Big Thicket
National Park. The bill died quietly in committee, without
anyone being the wiser as to why it was introduced. On June 10
the second House hearing on the Big Thicket was held in
Beaumont. It was very nearly a carbon copy of the first hearing,
with one exception. In March, 1972, the National Park Service,
in a move remarkable for its sheer blindness, sent out a mailing
to over 100 area homeowners in areas being considered for
inclusion in a Big Thicket Park. The letters warned that local
property might be confiscated by the government, and that if so
the government would pay full market value for all property and
provide relocation assistance.

In the end, only a tiny handful of homeowners were to be
moved from their residences for the sake of Big Thicket conservation. But the result of the Park Service mailout was to be,
predictably, a torrent of protest; protest, and the formation of
the Save Our Homes and Land Committee, which was to testify
heatedly at the coming June hearings. Conservationists and
Congressmen explained at length that every effort would be
made (as it was made) to keep from including homesites in the

preserve. The damage, however, was done. Local resistance to the park, formerly non-existent, was now loud and determined. Conservationists wondered whether they had more to fear from the lumber companies or from the National Park Service.

In November, 1972, Congressman John Dowdy, still under indictment, lost his congressional seat to State Senator Charles Wilson of Lufkin. This removed one obstinate obstacle to conservation. But it produced a new set of ground rules. Congressman Wilson was able to live with the idea of a Big Thicket National Park. But he would insist on doing so on his own terms. And his own terms involved the creation of a park which left out the Big Sandy-Village Creek Corridor with its homesites, and which allowed the lumber interests to feel that if they had not won the Big Thicket dispute, they had at least headed off the worst possible outcome.

Wilson hoped to resolve things quickly, ending a quarrel which had produced increasing bitterness on both sides. In spite of his determined efforts, however, the clumsy process of legislation and counter-legislation was to continue for nearly two more years. There is no point in trying to cover all of this in detail here. If what has been described so far is only a sketch, what follows will be only a bare outline. Those interested in detailed accounts should read James J. Cozine's PhD dissertation "Assault on a Wilderness" (1976) and Joe C. Wells' thesis "The Big Thicket Association" (1981), specifics of which are given in the bibliography.

Enter 1973. In January, Senator Bentsen introduced S.314 to create a 100,000-acre park. This was quickly followed by new congressman Dale Milford's 100,000-acre H.R.4270, and by the reintroduction of Bob Eckhardt's H.R.5941: his detailed bill for 100,000 acres, this time fatefully titled to create not a national park but a national biological preserve. Virtually all of this activity reaffirmed positions achieved in the previous session of Congress.

This, however, was to change. On June 13, Congressman Wilson redefined the situation by introducing a bill for a national park of 75,000 acres, larger than the "string of pearls" but minuscule compared to the "wheel of green." It was clearly a compromise between what the lumber interests wanted and what the conservationists preferred. But since Wilson was now the congressman from the district containing the park-to-be, his preference was going to be heard.

Against him were arrayed nearly all the other pieces of legislation and their sponsors. On the day prior to the unveiling of Wilson's bill, Senator Tower had introduced S.1981, his 100,000-acre Biological Reserve bill. On July 12, newly elected Republican Congressman from Dallas, Alan Steelman, introduced H.R.9051 to create a 74,746 acre Biological Preserve. Steelman's alliance with Charles Wilson was short-lived, however. On July 28, he proposed H.R.9253, describing a 100,000-acre area. Steelman was not the congressman from the Big Thicket district, but he was well-placed. A member of the powerful House Interior Committee, he had convinced all eleven committee members to cosign both his bills.

With five bills now pending, yet a third House hearing was held in Washington, D.C., on July 16-17. This was to be a near repeat of previous Congressional hearings, with one exception: a National Park Service recommendation of a 68,000-acre park. The N.P.S. recommendation consisted of Wilson's bill, minus the Neches River and Little Pine Island corridors, which the congressman insisted were necessary for recreational use. The N.P.S. 68,000-acre proposal was soon incarnated in a piece of legislation, S.2286, introduced on July 30 by senators Henry "Scoop" Jackson and Paul Fannin. With Steelman's legislation, this made seven bills pending. And no means on the horizon to unpend them.

All sides—besides being sick and tired of the endless legislative wrangle—now faced a quandary. Something had to be done to end the log jam. The struggle to save some significant remnant of the Big Thicket had gone on for nearly ten years now. With bad luck it might continue for yet another decade. Distasteful as this prospect appeared, it was clear also that any means of breaking the stalemate would upset some constituency—perhaps all. Even Wilson's 75,000 acres were more than the lumber interests found acceptable. To conservationists, who had compromised and recompromised, each time losing acreage they considered irreplaceable, Wilson's bill seemed too little, too late. Still, something had to be done.

On October 5, 1973, Congressman Bob Eckhardt and Congressman Charles Wilson held a joint press conference announcing a compromise. It had not been arrived at easily. From the House hearings through early fall, debates, protestations, and every kind of negotiation had gone on behind the scenes. The result—an 84,550-acre Big Thicket National Preserve—was agreed to by the lumber interests at the urging of Arthur Temple, Jr. It was also agreed to by most conservationists: or at any rate by their leaders. With legislators, ecologists, and lumber interests in agreement, Congress finally moved. With the entire Texas delegation as cosigners, H.R.11546 passed the U.S. House of Representatives on December 4.

At last, through a thousand shocks and frictions, sweet Reason had prevailed, and a final resolution of the Big Thicket debate was at hand. Or so it seemed. All that was needed was for the Senate to pass a companion bill to H.R.11546. The President was sure to sign it. And the nation's first national biological preserve would be a reality.

But on the very next day Senator Lloyd Bentsen introduced H.R.11546 to create a preserve not of 84,550 but of 100,000-acres! The difference between the House and the Senate bills was the 16,450 acre Big Sandy-Village Creek Corridor, long coveted by conservationists, which bound together two preserve units (Big Sandy and Turkey Creek) and attached them to the Neches River Corridor. Arguably the best canoeing stream in East Texas, Big Sandy-Village Creek was the heart of both George Bush's bill and of Bob Eckhardt's "wheel of green." It contained a wide variety of vegetation, including the "arid sandland" association, remarkable for semidesert soils and plants not contained extensively elsewhere in the Preserve.

The introduction of Bentsen's bill shattered a none-too-solid conservationist consensus. Both the Big Thicket Association and the Big Thicket Coordinating Committee reversed their previous positions and moved to embrace the forbidden creek corridor. Congressman Wilson—quite correctly, in fact—felt that he had been betrayed by the conservationist leaders who had sworn to support him. Senator Bentsen—correct, at least in the short run—felt that he had the upper hand. On February 5-6, the second Senate hearing on the Big Thicket was held in Washington, D.C., and on May 30 the Senate passed Bentsen's H.R.11546, a 100,000-acre bill containing the disputed Big Sandy-Village Creek Corridor. Conservationists were elated. Congressman Wilson, not unexpectedly, protested bitterly against the new legislation and insisted that 84,500 acres was as big a preserve as ever would exist in the Big Thicket.

Then there was a long, dull silence. Usually when the U.S. House and Senate pass contrasting versions of the same legislation the result is a House-Senate Conference Committee which attempts to iron out the differences between the two approaches. A conference committee can be called into session immediately after passage of the second (usually the Senate) bill. Or there may be a wait, while the two factions work out their differences in private. In the case of the Big Thicket, as spring moved into summer and summer towards fall, no middle ground could be reached. Nothing happened, day after day.

There is a quaint piece of unwritten legislation in the U.S. Congress. If a Congressman opposes a piece of legislation which directly and uniquely affects his district, his opposition stands. The legislation in question will not get out of committee; or if it gets out of committee the House will not pass it. (A similar "courtesy" exists in the U.S. Senate, where the existence of two senators representing each state complicates things. Even so, a single senator can usually veto a bill directly affecting his or her state.)

As week dragged after week that summer, conservationists began to take seriously Congressman Wilson's adamant assertion that either Congress would accept his bill *or there would be no bill*: there would be no Big Thicket National Preserve. It had been ten years since the founding of the second Big Thicket Association, four years since passage of the first abortive Big Thicket Legislation—four years and an almost endless series of debates and counterdebates. It was, as one ecologist complained, like an endless political campaign without an election.

Should it all be given up now as lost? Or should conservationists swallow the bitter pill and compromise once and for all?

The result was a foregone conclusion. In August the Big Thicket Association, along with the other members of the Big Thicket Coordinating Committee, met with Congressman Wilson and agreed—again, but this time with finality—to accept the 84,550-acre compromise. The logjam was now, finally, broken. Instead of calling a conference committee, the House Interior Committee simply redrafted Wilson's bill. On September 24, the full House passed the legislation and sent it to the Senate. Both Senators Bentsen and Tower accepted the compromise, which passed the Senate on October 1 without dissent. On October 11, 1974, ten years after the struggle first began in a rural church in Saratoga, Texas, President Gerald Ford signed a bill establishing the Big Thicket National Preserve.

To the average citizen nothing could be more clear. To create a national park one simply sets aside an area and keeps bulldozers and real estate developers out. Or, if people are let in, they are to be allowed only in certain places and kept out of others. The rest is up to Mother Nature.

In fact, things are more complex—more complex, and far more difficult—than this bright image suggests. What follows is an account of the establishing of the Big Thicket National Preserve. It is, like the description of the legislative process, intended to be brief and to the point.

One of the most intractable obstacles to saving a portion of the Thicket was, at first, no more clear to those who were trying to save it than to the Park Service. This was the first potential addition to the Park Service to be justified on the basis of biology alone. The underlying problem was therefore one of reconceiving the very nature of conservation: a problem which required many years of groping to resolve. Though the Thicket may have had historical, recreational, and aesthetic values, the fundamental rationale was to be ecology, pure and simple. This was a new idea: to save every moss, every fern, every fungus, every orchid, every vine, every insect—that is, every native species—and their interrelations, however subtle. Like most new ideas, it was ahead of its time. It was hard, at first, to grasp.

It was also going to be hard to put into effect. The National Park Service looked on the Preserve's long stream corridors and isolated units with foreboding. Could they be policed? Would they be biologically self-sustaining? Or would they require constant managing, even supposing management practices like burning, replanting, and restocking could succeed in saving all species and their interrelations? Equally puzzling were special provisions which, even at the end, had to be written into the Big Thicket bill in order to secure its passage. Hunting was to be allowed—by permit only and not in all areas. Oil exploration and drilling were to be allowed: by special permit and under environmental restrictions. Even if these were to pose no serious problems—which seemed more than a little over-optimistic—there was still the question of how many and what sort of trails and roads to allow in the preserve, what sort of preserve headquarters to project and build, whether to keep some sensitive areas off limits to all but a few researchers, and how precisely to draw the Preserve's boundaries.

As if these problems were not enough, there loomed a still larger one. When the House committee redrafted Congressman Wilson's bill immediately prior to its passage, it cut out a "legislative taking" provision that would have put all lands instantly inside preserve boundaries under federal control. The result was dangerous. In order to take control of land in the preserve, the National Park Service would have to buy it, a parcel at a time. To do this it was going to have to get funding from Congress, also a piece at a time, and to institute legal proceedings in those cases where owners did not accept the (rather ample) offers made by the Park Service.

This produced two difficulties. The first—less serious—was that the actual preserve would take years to materialize. In this case, in fact, it took eighteen years before the last piece of land was purchased. The second—very serious indeed—was that before it could be protected, land intended for the preserve might be clearcut or otherwise mangled. That could happen especially if an owner should decide to "spite cut," i.e. to cut "his" forest in revenge for its being taken into the Preserve. Or it could happen through misplaced or mishandled attempts to control infestations of the Southern pine bark beetle. Or it could happen if economic pressures forced a landowner to cut his forests before the Federal Government could buy them.

To their credit, the large lumber companies cut no trees within the preserve's boundaries, though such abstinence involved real sacrifices. Kirby Industries alone paid over $117,000 in taxes from 1967 through 1976 on land it held within the preserve. In another instance Temple-Eastex announced in March, 1974, that it would not cut a 410-acre tract of timber that it had purchased before realizing it would be inside the preserve. "We paid $34,000 dollars for the timber," stated Arthur Temple, Jr., chairman of Temple-Eastex (now Temple-Inland), "but we would rather lose the money than cut the trees."

It was unfortunate that all those involved in the new preserve could not take Temple's enlightened view. The National Park Service estimated that in the first few months of the Big Thicket National Preserve's existence, approximately 2500 to 3000 acres of forest in the preserve were destroyed by small timber operators, real estate developers, and pine beetle salvage operations attempting to control the pine beetle by cutting all pine trees in and around infested areas. Conservationists set the figure higher, at nearly 4000 acres, and pointed to the destruction of nearly one-fourth of the Beech Creek Unit (2000 of its 8000 acres) by beetle control and salvage operations.

It is fortunate that this sudden onslaught slowed, or the preserve would soon have become a national grassland. Adverse publicity from conservationists, along with quickly engineered land purchases by the park service, headed off what would have been a debacle. In 1976 funds were found by Senator Bentsen and Congressman Wilson to buy 6000 acres of "endangered tracts" in the preserve. The move came not a moment too soon. Only foresightful maneuvering by William Jewell, in charge of Thicket land purchase for the park service, prevented the cutting of additional hundreds of acres.

Meanwhile, endless planning and policy decisions had to be made, all requiring public input, all requiring public discussion. There were to be nearly as many of these as there had been pieces of Big Thicket legislation: boundary descriptions, an environmental statement, a visitors' use and general development plan, a land acquisition plan, regulations on oil and gas activities, wilderness hearings, a general management plan, a resource management plan, and so on.

Conservationists, deeply engaged in all of these projects, wryly conceded that they had gone from a legislative tangle into a bureaucratic morass. But better the bureaucracy, they admitted, than the loss of the Big Thicket. Out of all of this, however, came one shining, non-bureaucratic achievement, based on the work of Billy Hallmon, a long-time Thicket enthusiast.

When the Big Thicket National Preserve was signed into law, its boundaries were described only in the most general terms. No specific landlines existed. So Billy Hallmon, weekend after weekend, drove down from Dallas and *walked the boundaries of the Preserve units, mapping/creating them step by step, mile after mile*, taking in an oxbow here, a seep there, leaving out a residence or a weekend cabin, keeping within the acreage limits of corridors and units, with no more equipment than a handheld map roller, a topo map, and an ankle-attached yardage gauge. No one asked him to do this, or paid him, or encouraged him. So far as I know, no one even thanked him.

But when the National Park Service—always short on funding and personnel—finally moved to establish preserve boundaries, they found themselves compelled either to accept Billy's maps or to wait one, two, three years for other ones. They accepted Billy Hallmon's boundaries—no doubt with due oversight and serious reflection—but they accepted them. Nor has anyone that I have heard of ever complained about them. If this is not an example of successful citizen participation, I wonder what is.

Meanwhile conservationists set out after a new goal: a Big Thicket State Park or set of parks. The national biological preserve was created to protect ecology, they argued. But there is also a need for tourism in the region. State parks were needed in the Big Thicket region not only for tourism and hence for the local economy, but also to shield the Big Thicket National Preserve from visitor pressure. Probably the loudest and most effective voice raised on behalf of the idea of creating a state park was Senator Ralph Yarborough, now retired in Austin, who continued to speak out for conservation. So effective were the Senator and his conservationist allies that by 1978 a several thousand acre Big Thicket State Park seemed a real possibility.

But that—considering the convoluted history of conservation in the region—would have been too easy. Not surprisingly, conservationists had picked out large tracts on Village Creek for the park site. After all, it was a beautiful creek, affording both recreational possibilities and a chance to conserve a diverse ecology. It was also, unfortunately, the area that Congressman Wilson had sworn to protect from government intrusion, an area containing homesites which, he had promised, would never be taken. Not one more acre would be amputated from Hardin County, he had orated. The people had nothing to fear. Now, confronted with a new conservationist aggression, he had to make good on his pledge.

There was only one way in the congressman's possession to block the state park: he could withhold land purchase funds from the Big Thicket Preserve, threatening to block them permanently until the conservationists relented. As always, Wilson acted decisively. A headline on the front page of the May 25, 1978 *Houston Chronicle* proclaimed WILSON PUTS HIS FOOT DOWN. If conservationists did not desist from trying to get a Village Creek State Park, he insisted, there would be no more funding for the Preserve. True to his word, Wilson cut 6.38 million dollars from preserve funding for the fiscal year 1979, leaving barely enough money for planning and legal work.

Once again conservationists were impaled on the horns of a dilemma. If they gave in, there would be no state park; if they persisted, there would be no national preserve. Luckily, the dilemma resolved itself. Texas State Parks and Wildlife found a willing seller: a citizen of Hardin County anxious to sell his land along Village Creek and perfectly glad to see it made into a park. Happily, it contained no homesites. The congressman, having put his foot down, could now pick it up. In October, 1979, a 926.7-acre state park site was acquired on Village Creek south of Silsbee, just east of Lumberton. The citizens of Lumberton even seemed to like the idea. It put their town on the map, and promised to boost its economy. Funding for the Preserve could now begin again.

A cloud of irony hung over the struggle for a state park on Village Creek. The national preserve already contained three portions of the Big Sandy-Village Creek through their inclusion in the Big Sandy, Turkey Creek, and Neches Corridor Units. The state park made a fourth ecological enclave on the disputed stream corridor—in fact, a fifth. Two years before purchase of the state park site, a still larger area—the Roy E. Larsen Sandyland Sanctuary—was created on Village Creek west of Silsbee. (The state park is south of that metropolis.) It was donated to the Nature Conservancy, a private nonprofit organization, by Temple-Eastex and Time, Inc. The moving force behind this gift was Arthur Temple, Jr.

The rationale for this gift is clear. The Big Thicket National Preserve contains, besides its stream corridors, samples of every sort of ecosystem found in the Big Thicket except one. That one, in a way, is the most unique and unexpected of the Thicket's subregions: the arid sandland association. With the exclusion of the Big Sandy-Village Creek Corridor from the preserve, the arid sandlands were left unprotected. Clearly, the Big Thicket ecological project was incomplete.

The Larsen Sanctuary's 2138 acres front on eight miles of Village Creek, running from FM 418 on the north to FM 327 on the south. Because of its location on these roads, it provides excellent put-in and take-out places for canoes and an easy, less-than-one-day float trip down the creek. Though part of its acreage consists of stream flood plain and baygall, most consists of one to three hundred feet deep sandy soils and the dryland plant associations which flourish on them. Over 550 plant species have been identified in this sanctuary; four are endangered, fifteen "state significant," and twelve uncommon in southeast Texas (most being West Texas plants somehow lost in the Piney Woods). In the words of Robert W. Parvin:

> Botanists now taking a closer look at the preserve's baygalls, ponds, and water-fed forests, which have been left undisturbed for a decade, are starting to

identify plant species heretofore unknown at Sandyland and, in some cases, in Texas. [Steve] Orzell and fellow botanist Edwin Bridges have documented sedges, yellow-eyed grasses, a summer-flowering lobelia, a carnivorous purple bladderwort, and a few other water-loving species. Yet another plant was an especially surprising find: Mohlenbrock's umbrella sedge (*Cyperus grayiodes*), a species under review for federal listing that was originally described as endemic to sand prairies along the Illinois River in Illinois.

In one respect environmentalists are surprised by each of these "finds." In another, of course, they are not surprised at all. The Big Thicket has always been the home of the unexpected.

I said that the Larsen Sanctuary contains 2138 acres. That was its original acreage, but, happily, it has grown. In 1978 Gulf States Utilities donated a forty-acre abandoned power line right of way to the sanctuary. In 1985 Sun Oil donated a ninety- six-and-a-half-acre tract containing a wetland and a "succession pond." In 1991 Temple-Inland (formerly Temple-Eastex) donated eighty acres, primarily frontage along FM 418. Purchase by Nature Conservancy of smaller tracts in 1990 and 1991 brings the total to just under 2400 acres. Also, a "ground lease" from Temple-Inland on the west bank of Village Creek adds approximately seven hundred acres to this total—all in all a sizeable, manageable sanctuary. (Needless to say, most environmentalists think this area should eventually become part of the Big Thicket National Preserve. But they are too delighted with its sheer existence now to protest about who owns it.)

In the decade-long campaign to create the Big Thicket National Preserve, conservationists said many bitter things about the lumber companies, many of which cut deeply. In the light of the Larsen Sanctuary, those remarks need to be reconsidered. At the very least they need to be balanced by the realization that far-sighted and public-spirited thinking is not alien to the timber interests. The Sandylands Preserve is living proof that this is so.

In preparing to write the present sketch, I compiled a chronological list (on an immense pad of drafting paper) of important events affecting Big Thicket conservation from 1966 through the present. There were, up through the dedication of the Larsen Preserve on April 16, 1977, one hundred and three of these (to which another twenty or thirty could easily have been added). From the dedication until the present I counted ninety-two: the opening of hiking trails in preserve units, the completion of studies and hearings, the gradual rise of visitation figures, the selection of a preserve headquarters site, the securing of land purchase funds. Out of this cornucopia of events I would like to stress only three: the selection of the Thicket as a "Man and the Biosphere Reserve," the deauthorization of dams on the Neches River, and Congressman Charles Wilson's sudden about-face on the issue of the Big Sandy-Village Creek Corridor.

The rationale of those who attempted to save something of the Big Thicket has always been uniqueness. Because of its blend of tropical and temperate, eastern and western, because of its legends and its remoteness, the Big Thicket, they have argued, is unique. They might also have argued, as did the Man and the Biosphere program, that it is representative, and worth saving on that account.

The Man and the Biosphere Program (MAB) is relatively new. It was launched in 1971 and designated its first reserves in 1976. A component of UNESCO (United Nations Educational, Scientific, and Cultural Organization), its viewpoint is worldwide. According to Kenton R. Miller, its diverse goals are:

> ... to conserve for present and future use the diversity and integrity of biotic communities of plants and animals within natural ecosystems, and to safeguard the genetic diversity of species on which their continuing evolution depends;
>
> ... to provide areas for ecological and environmental research including, particularly, baseline studies both

within and adjacent to such reserves, such research to be consistent with the above objective;

. . . to provide facilities for education and training.

In other words, the Man and the Biosphere Reserves are an attempt to save significant portions of each of the world's "biogeographic provinces" (its basic ecological areas) and to learn how to manage them so that they can sustain both themselves and support their surrounding ecosystems. MAB reserves have another goal, namely, to help solve problems in the relations between people and the environment, *to the lasting advantage of both*. (In a way, the Man and the Biosphere Program tries to do for the world what the Big Thicket National Preserve tries to do for Southeast Texas: to save representative samples of each major ecosystem and manage these for the benefit of both nature and its human inhabitants. It is interesting that both MAB and the BTNP were hatched in the same years, in response to similar problems.)

On October 2, 1981, the Executive Bureau of UNESCO's MAB Program approved the Big Thicket National Preserve for inclusion in its global network of biosphere reserves. It was to function, the executive bureau stated, as part of an international interdisciplinary program intended to improve management of the world's resources. Of the Programs's 210 reserves, 37 were in the United States and 15 were managed by the National Park Service. The designation of the Big Thicket Preserve as a biosphere reserve not only substantiates the claims which conservationists have made for its biological richness, it also supports their arguments that this richness and diversity are very useful.

The research, correspondence, and persistent advocacy which won international MAB status for the Big Thicket were undertaken not by the Sierra Club or the Big Thicket Coordinating Committee, but by the Stephen F. Austin State University School of Forestry. (That's right: School of *Forestry*.) Not only are the foresters thus due a vote of thanks; they are due an open mind, and freedom from some of the stereotypes which environmentalists too often foist upon them.

Village Creek

If one looks into the details of the Man and the Biosphere designation, one discovers that the "biogeographic province" which includes the Thicket preserve is the Austroriparian Province. What this means is unclear—at any rate, in spite of much reading I could find no definition of it—until one looks at a map. Then one sees that the outlines of the Austroriparian Province fit snugly over those of the Southeastern Evergreen Forest. That is, the most representative deep Southern forest of the United States turns out to be not in Mississippi or the Carolinas, but in the southern state which appears to be least southern of all: Texas.

The designation of the Big Thicket as a Man and the Biosphere Reserve came as welcome news to both conservationists and the Park Service. Unfortunately it could not resolve certain gnawing problems created by the preserve's very structure. Of all the areas in the National Park Service, the Big Thicket National Preserve is the only one containing widely dispersed, separated units. This has always been a matter of concern for both conservationists and the Park Service. Can such isolated areas survive by themselves, their ecosystems intact? Can they sustain the plant species for which they merited protection in the first place? There are two reasons why these questions have been rendered especially acute. The first is that many lumber companies, since the creation of the preserve, have with few exceptions continued to clearcut *right up to the fencelines of the preserve units*. In these areas no "buffer zones" have been allowed to exist, with even a scattering of hardwoods, to make a transition. The various units have, with few exceptions, become islands of diverse vegetation in a sea of pine monoculture.

But islands do not always do well. Since the creation of the Preserve a new subspecialty of ecology has flowered, and has entered the public mind. It is called "island biogeography," and it teaches that the smaller the isolated area (the smaller the island) the fewer species it will support. A great deal could be said about island biogeography. Its root equation, (a 50 percent decrease in land area leads to a 10 percent loss in number of species), has held up well in research on islands. Whether a preserve unit, or for that matter a national park, is in the fullest sense an "island" is arguable. A deer can walk through pine plantation to get to a preserve unit; it cannot swim the Pacific to get to Hawaii. Still, island biogeography casts a somber light on all disjunct natural areas, and strongly suggests that they will survive better if they are integrally related to their surrounding ecology. This realization is built strongly into the Man and the Biosphere program, one of whose central goals is to try to learn how to imbed nature reserves into their biogeographical contexts so as to both support the context and to guarantee their own existence.

In the case of the Thicket preserve, the obvious thread needed to bind things together and interrelate otherwise unrelated units is the long-disputed Big Sandy-Village Creek Corridor. Protection of this corridor assures that the Big Sandy Creek Unit, the Turkey Creek Unit, and the Lower Neches River Corridor Unit would be interrelated, not to mention the Nature Conservancy's Sandland Preserve and the Village Creek State Park. One could guarantee that these areas would not be isolated—that birds, game animals, and plant species could continue to circulate between them. But there has been bitter controversy over this area in the past, to no effect. Better to turn one's energies elsewhere, to issues that need facing and about which one might succeed in actually accomplishing something.

That is what conservationists did. They left Village Creek to one side and set out to protect the Preserve in another way. By persistent efforts, which included press releases, political pressure and organizing local landowners, conservationists were able to get two potential dams on the Neches River "deauthorized"—that is, taken off the U.S. Corps of Engineers' list of dams to be built and bottomlands to be drowned. The first, Dam A, would have been built in the middle of the Neches River Corridor of the Thicket preserve. Not only would it have destroyed a canoeing stream, but it also would have diminished the land base of lumber companies by tens of thousands of acres and buried two Preserve units. The second, the Rockland Dam and Reservoir on the upper Neches River, would have done the same. It would also have displaced several hundred local residents and destroyed vast acreages of now-rare hardwood bottomlands. When the Rockland project was deauthorized in November 1988, conservationists and local people both had reason to celebrate. They were not the only ones who could have celebrated. The two dams were economic boondoggles. No argument could justify them on economic grounds. They would have been pork barrel projects.

Meanwhile, there was Big Sandy-Village Creek. In June, 1986, one of Congressman Charles Wilson's aides began calling Texas conservationists asking their opinion about adding 14,000 acres to the Big Thicket National Preserve, including Village Creek. The first response of conservationists was: Are we hearing right? Which Creek? You want Village Creek? In Texas? Yes, said the aide: Would you consider adding it to the Preserve?

Well: Would you consider winning the state lottery, if you had just bought fifty tickets? Conservationists allowed as how they just might consider adding the creek corridor to the Preserve. Of course, they would have to think about it. They thought very hard. In September they brought out a proposal, including Big Sandy Creek—from the Big Sandy Unit to the Turkey Creek Unit to the Neches River Corridor; a small Lower Neches Unit on the east side of the Neches at its confluence with Village Creek; a "Canyonlands" Unit on the high country west of the Neches just below Dam B. On October 2, 1986, Congressman Wilson introduced H.R.5646 to add Village Creek Corridor (7000 acres) to the Big Thicket National Preserve and 7000 acres to widen the Neches River Corridor. Almost exactly a year later the Congressman decided to amend his bill (now H.R.3544). On October 22, 1987, he proposed an addition of 13,920 acres including Big Sandy Corridor, Village Creek Corridor, and the Canyonlands Unit.

Conceivably, this bill could have sailed through Congress and received a presidential signature in a matter of months. Those who have read this book up to this point, however, will know better. The course of conservation in the Big Thicket never did run smooth, and the "Big Thicket Addition" was to be no exception. There was to be a local hearing (May 21, 1988) and then a House hearing in Washington, D.C., (July 14, 1988); and then—since one hearing is *never* enough—yet another D.C. House hearing (June 13, 1989). And then a Senate hearing (October 24, 1989) in D.C. In the meantime there would be every kind of political infighting, involving both local homeowners on Village Creek (who were guaranteed they would not lose their homesites through creation of the corridor) and Senator Phil Gramm (R.-Tex.) who at first seemed to want to veto the Addition Bill, only to reverse his stance when concessions were made.

But by now the reader must be as tired of reading about political squabbles as I am of writing about them. The Big Thicket Addition Bill—along with other potential additions to conservation in the Thicket region—will be discussed again in the last chapter of this book, on the future of conservation in the Big Thicket Region. In the meantime, one would be more than justified in asking: But what is there *now*? What hiking trails and canoe trips and horseback rides actually exist? How does one get there, and can I take my Sunday school, or my Girl Scout troop? The answers to these questions, and a few more, are provided in the next chapter, on The Big Thicket Now.

6

The Big Thicket Now: A Users' Guide

Often, in the management of national parks and monuments, the time comes when overuse of trails and camping areas becomes destructive. This has raised problems for the National Park Service most notably in Yellowstone and Yosemite, but also in the less remote areas of the Great Smoky Mountains National Park—to name only a few cases. In the Thicket, nothing could be farther from the truth. The Big Thicket is, and until now has remained, one of the most under-utilized resources in the National Park Service.

In part, the reasons for this stem from the history of the preserve. Because twenty years were required for the purchase of all its lands, there were few complete Park Service controlled preserve units to visit for the first ten years. Even when units were purchased, it often proved impossible to build and maintain trails. The Ronald Reagan years had come, and funds for the Park Service were few and far between.

Gradually both of these factors have been eased. This is not to say that the Park Service is not woefully understaffed, or that further campsites and trails are not needed. But today there are plenty of trails to hike, deep woods drives to drive, and canoe trips to float. Plenty of places to birdwatch, or surprise a deer in the late evening light, or just to sit quietly and put oneself together. Or picnic. Or, in some places, to swim.

What follows is a tour of the "Accessible Big Thicket": places anyone can get to, and enjoy, most of them without even

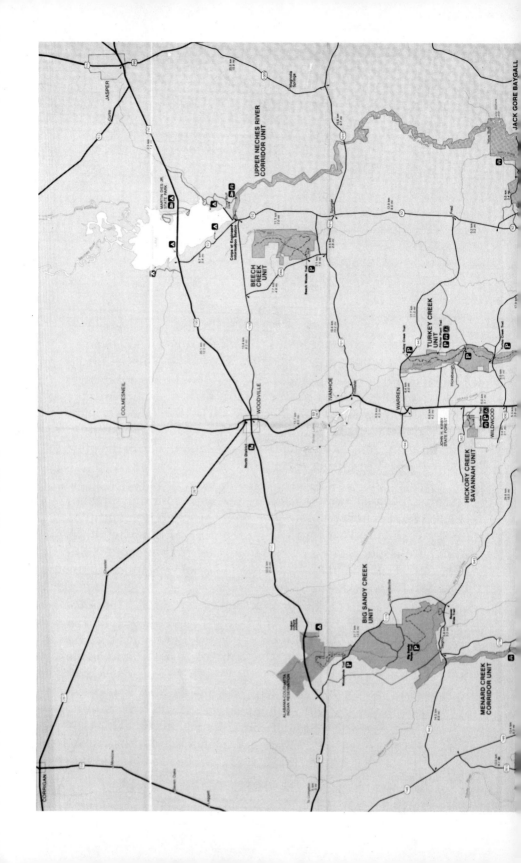

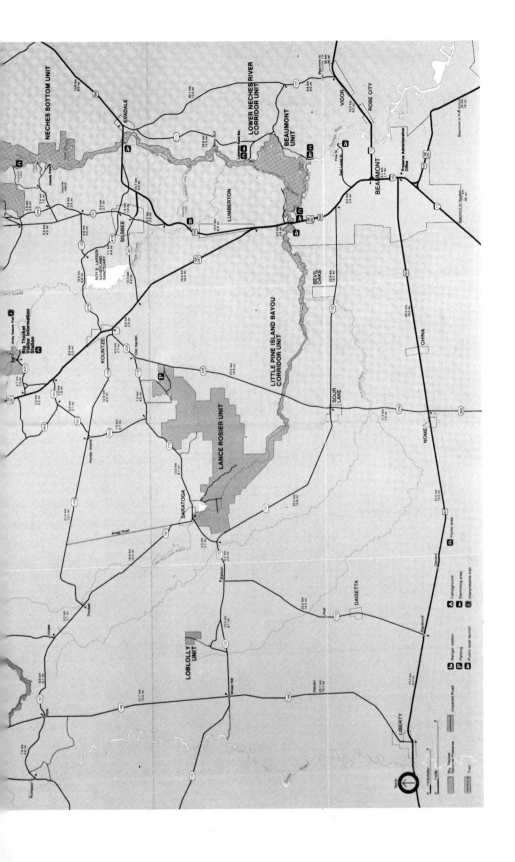

NECHES BOTTOM UNIT

EVADALE

LOWER NECHES RIVER
CORRIDOR UNIT

BEAUMONT
UNIT

VIDOR

ROSE CITY

Preserve Administrative
Office

BEAUMONT

LUMBERTON

SILSBEE

ROY E. LARSEN
SANDYLAND
SANCTUARY

BEVIL
OAKS

Big Thicket
Visitor Information
Station

KOUNTZE

LITTLE PINE ISLAND BAYOU
CORRIDOR UNIT

CHINA

Old Hardin

Honey Island

SOUR
LAKE

LANCE ROSIER UNIT

NOME

SARATOGA

Bragg Road

Batson

DAISETTA

Thicket

LOBLOLLY
UNIT

Moss Hill

Hardin

LIBERTY

North

Big Thicket
National Preserve

Unpaved Road

Ranger station

Parking

Public boat launch

Campground

Swimming area

Interpretive trail

Picnic area

getting mud on one's feet (even if it does rain). There are eleven preserve units. Their resources will be explored one at a time, starting with the southwestern quadrant of the Preserve and ending in the northeast: that is, beginning at the Rosier Unit and finishing at Beech Creek. After this journey it will be time to talk about canoe trips, which are mostly between, but not in, units. And about some nature areas that are not in the preserve. Happily, maps will be provided throughout.

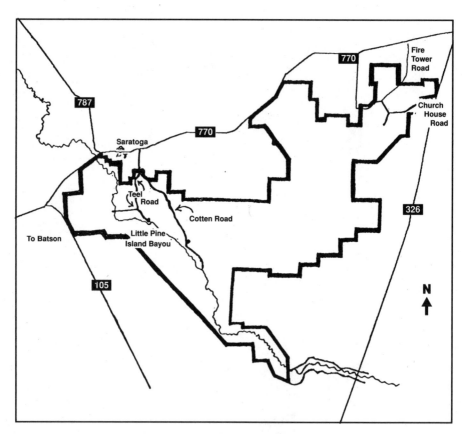

Lance Rosier Unit

Lance Rosier Unit: Driving and Primitive Hiking

Largest of the preserve segments, at 24,942 acres, the Lance Rosier Unit contains a wide diversity of ecological communities, but does not now boast any marked trails—a condition that will eventually be remedied. The lack of trails is made up for, however, by fine back country driving on sandy roads. The longest of these is on the Cotten Road, which turns south off Highway 770, nine-tenths of a mile east of the post office in Saratoga. Beginning in the old oil field, the Cotten Road soon leaves the litter of rusted oil storage tanks, piping, and pumps, and then tunnels under a dense green canopy of pine-hardwood forest. Trending gradually southeastward, it ends 4.6 miles from the highway at Little Pine Island Bayou. Along the bayou are some massive cypress that somehow escaped cutting. The two largest measure sixteen and nineteen feet in circumference, respectively. At that size they are probably three or four centuries old. They were ancient when the first white men foraged into East Texas.

There are at least three features along the Cotten Road worth exploring. The first (1.5 miles from the highway) is Kinky Branch: an incredibly looping, small waterfilled creek that meanders under big beech trees, magnolias, and pines, almost rejoining itself a dozen times before it empties into Little Pine Island Bayou. The second (a mile farther) is off the road to the east, just past a pipeline right-of-way: Buck Pond, a flatwoods pond supporting a forest of water tupelo, mayhaw, and water oak. Three and seven-tenths miles from the highway, on the left, stands a gigantic live oak, planted by the father of Lance Rosier, the home-grown conservationist, for whom the unit is named. The trunk of this tree is at least six feet in diameter at shoulder level, and its branches, any one of which is as large as a good-sized tree, are matted with moss and sensitive fern. Nearby stands a big white oak also planted by the Rosiers. Environmentalists insist a log cabin should be built here as a memorial to Lance, who was born and grew up at this spot.

The Cotten Road is actually more complex than this account makes it seem. Rather than running straight and single into the middle of the unit, it divides only seven-tenths of a mile south of Highway 770. The Cotten Road *per se* continues south by southeast; the right fork, called the Teel Road, continues south and west, 1.3 of a mile later itself forking, the left fork soon ending (one-tenth of a mile) at the old Teel Cemetery. The right fork slopes gradually down for a little over a mile (1.2 miles) ending at a concrete bridge over Little Pine Island Bayou. The bridge is closed to traffic, but it makes a good fishing place, or simply a good vantage point from which to watch turtles hanging suspended in tea-colored water, or wading birds stalking or soaring over the forest overhang: a point of high meditation.

Beyond the bridge there are three choices for hiking. If water is low one can hike north along the bayou on wooded flats between the water on one side and the palmetto jungle on the other. Or one can hike straight ahead up the old road, which, though grown up in weeds, is still passable. The more adventurous can follow a trail to the left, between a cypress slough that feeds into the bayou and a pond grown up in waterweeds and willows and dead trees. The last time I made this turn I was greeted by an armadillo, two different kinds of ducks (the brush was too thick for identification), a Louisiana heron and a great blue heron. All, including the armadillo, made quick exits. It would have been interesting to stay and find out what fifth species of water bird had flown up into the willows and remained there, making a strange plaintive cry until I was halfway back across the bridge. It must have had a nest nearby.

The Teel Cemetery is a jewel: a beautifully kept rectangle of mown grass and marble and granite headstones under a high spreading canopy of magnolias, white oaks and loblolly pines. Most of the stones are for Teels, but there are a sprinkling of Mayos, Cottens and Roberts. One Teel was a Confederate soldier; a Mayo was a Lieutenant Colonel in the U.S. Air Force.

This area was to have been an interpretive center for the Park Service. The old Teel log cabin was here, built by slaves

Palmetto Thicket

before the Civil War. It was burned down—no one knows by whom—shortly before being acquired for the Preserve. The best bet now for an interpretive center is the site of the old Rosier home.

One more point of interest. Nine-tenths of a mile down Teel Road from its intersection with Cotten Road there is a swamp on the west side of the road. One of the pleasures of writing this book was, finally, to have a chance to wade across, and then hike around it.

On the east side, where it comes to within a few yards of Cotten Road, the area is a cypress swamp; to the west, before it turns into a blackwater pond, it becomes predominantly water tupelo.

It is a strange place: deadly silent. The water, nearly black in the afternoon light, is covered with a broken skin of small green plants that cluster together on the surface. Where sunslant breaks through, it is tea-colored and transparent down to a carpet of fallen leaves, branches, and waterweeds. No squirrels chatter there (though I did see one squirrel's nest high up, in the crown of a tupelo); no birds sing. There are no minnows in the water, and only a few water bugs play on the surface. I saw one frog, who eyed me in astonishment from a cypress knee, then plunged into the murk. No snake, no turtle, no fish disturbed the green mirror. Even the wind lay still.

I listened; far off, a cardinal piped. Crows called, their voices muted and warped almost past recognition in the hush. It felt like the beginning of time.

After an hour I emerged from the *Urphänomenon*, sweat-soaked and satisfied. For years I had wanted to explore that swamp, and now it was done.

One thing bothered me. That swamp is not natural. It is man-made. Beyond the blackwater pond at its western edge runs an old road, now abandoned, going back to forest. It makes a dam, holding back the water, making a swamp out of what would otherwise have been only a shallow, seepy creekbottom. I wonder if the lumber company that built the road realized it had created a swamp.

At any rate, the swamp can be seen from the road. Visitors do not have to creep through it, wondering if their next step will land on a turtle or a catfish. They can enjoy it from the car window.

The other drive in the Rosier Unit comes in not from the north, with the Cotten Road, but from the east, off State Highway 326. This is called the Church House or Rock Creek Road, and it heads into the unit 2.3 miles from the intersection of Highways 720 and 326 to the northeast, and 2.7 miles from the intersection of 326 and 105 to the southwest, in Sour Lake. (The mileage figures aren't necessary; the Church House Road leaves the highway just north of the clearly visible Little Rock Assembly of God Church, on the west side.)

Though the entire three miles of this drive lie within the Preserve, the first part runs through scruffy cutover country that looks too poor to be of biological value. One can only plead for patience. This acreage had to be taken in so that the Rosier Unit would form a single contiguous area. It will grow back in time, redeveloping into the upland longleaf pine savannah that it was originally. Within less than a mile the cutover lands are past, and a keen eye can spot the upland pine savannah species that define this area (waxmyrtle, buttonbush, titi, shortleaf and longleaf pine). Where the Church Creek Road deadends, the now abandoned Fire Tower Road—still hikeable—runs northeast through dry savannah. This would be a good place to stop and walk a little. Not far to the northeast, on the right hand side of the road, is a pitcher plant (*Sarracenia*) bog replete with club moss, with orchids in season (*Calapogon*) and two more insect eaters: terrestrial bladderwort and butterwort.

I suppose it would be anticlimactic to point out that this area is as different from the cypress swamps and palmetto jungles in the west and central portions of this unit as any two units in the Preserve are different from each other.

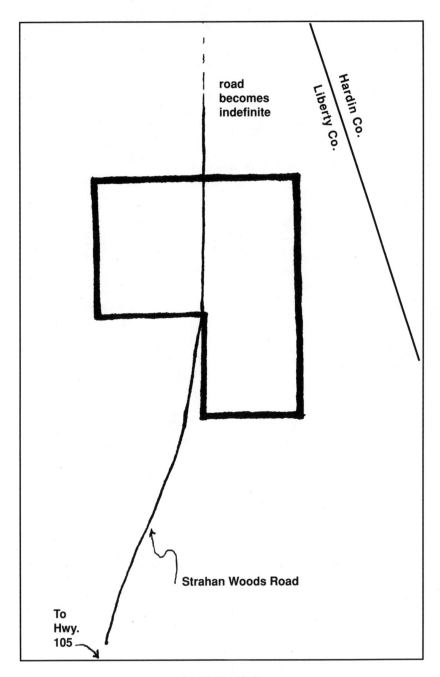

road
becomes
indefinite

Hardin Co.
Liberty Co.

Strahan Woods Road

To
Hwy.
105

Loblolly Unit

Loblolly Unit

The Loblolly Unit is a real oddity. Tied up in the courts from around the turn of the century through a contested will, it has never been cut by a lumber company. On the other hand, since in 1900 it was a relatively bald prairie, there were originally no trees to cut. When this area did forest over, it was primarily with the moisture-loving loblolly pine. One thus has here something almost unheard of in East Texas: virgin forest.

To get there take State Highway 105 west from Batson (5.1 miles) or east from Moss Hill (2.9 miles), across from Mt. Cavalry Baptist Church, and drive north 2.7 miles. The sand road enters the unit here, exiting seven-tenths of a mile later.

There are no trails in this unit. One can enjoy the drive, or one can get out and hike, finding one's own way. But if there are no trails, paradoxically there are also now very few loblolly pines. Most of the loblollies along the road have been cut to "control" infestations of the pine bark beetle, accelerating the ecological succession from prairie to pine to hardwood. Where found, the remaining pines are usually large (three to three-and-one-half feet in diameter shoulder high) and soaring (eighty-five to one hundred feet tall). The rest is sweetgum, swamp chestnut oak, red oak, water oak. There are a handful of swamps where tupelo rise from standing water among crawfish mounds. There are Christmas ferns and arrowwood and American holly.

There are also some Indian sites: round water-filled depressions nine to fifteen feet in diameter and three to six feet deep, which may have provided clay for pottery making. Sometimes two holes are found alongside each other with a ditch in between. It is speculated that when one depression was deepened it drew water off from the other, which allowed it—now water-free—to be mined further.

Menard Creek Corridor: The Confluence Trail Walk

The Confluence Trail is more a brisk walk than a hike. To get there take State Highway 747 west from Rye (or east from Cleveland). At Romayor, just east of the Trinity River, head north on Farm Road 2610. Three miles later take a left on Oak Hill Drive (next to the 6 Lakes Store) and another left on Forest Park Lane, which arrives at a primitive parking area on the right. The path opens out west from the parking, under the shade of sweetgum trees. A smell of pines hangs in the air.

The path soon splits. To the right it leads quickly to a picnic table under the black shade of oak and sweetgum trees and trailing rattan vines. Forty feet below, Menard Creek rolls lazily past half sunk logs populated by turtles. A path leads down to a bank from which many a bass or channel catfish has been caught over the years. White oaks two and three feet in diameter rise above the sweetgum and water oaks.

The left hand "y" runs along the top of a ridge, through a shady tunnel of maple and sweetgum. Finally it turns, facing the Trinity River. Here too there is a picnic table with benches. There is also a new wood fence along the crest of the hill, with a view of slow creek and broad, fast-moving river. Menard Creek here is probably fifty feet wide; the river is eighty yards in breadth at least; and beyond it lies a sandbar as wide as the river, stalked by herons.

This is a great place to eat, to fish, to watch the river. I judge the distance from the parking lot to the table as less than a half mile. The big trees here are cottonwoods: some of them four and five feet in diameter. They make a nice pattering sound in the wind.

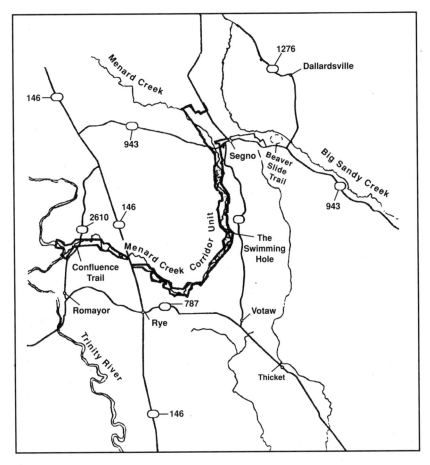

Menard Creek

Menard Creek Corridor: The Swimming Hole

On new maps of the Preserve, there is a picnic table marker about half way up the Menard Creek Corridor (5.4 miles north of the junction of FM 787 and FM 2798; 5.6 miles south of the junction of FM 2798 and FM 943). It doesn't look very promising. But appearances are misleading.

To get there turn west off FM 2798 onto a sandy road marked Holly Grove Baptist Church and Cemetery. The road crosses Menard Creek, and in the woods along the creek just north of the bridge there are daytime camping areas. On the west side stand two picnic tables with benches, and on the east three. On each side there are parking places and walking paths to the creek; on the east there is a public toilet.

The creek widens out here and deepens, making a natural swimming hole. When I was there fifteen youngsters were splashing in the cool, fast-moving water, watched by a sprinkling of adults. Someone had tied a rope to a cypress tree, and the braver kids were swinging on it and dropping with a loud kersplash. There is plenty of shade on the tables, and an open sandy view of the creek.

I am fascinated by the changeable character of Menard Creek here. For seventy-five yards it flows straight and deep, then for who-knows-how-many yards it loops and reloops, dividing, rejoining, making deep pools and then shallowing out with the sand ripples clearly visible: all under the dapple of deep shade and the constant dark interruption of vines and cypress knees.

There are unmarked trails down each side of the creek—made, one suspects, by local fishers.

Turkey Creek Unit: A Fifteen-Mile Trail

Though the Turkey Creek Trail is fifteen miles long from the south end of the unit to the north, it divides naturally into three segments. The first (six miles long) runs from the Visitor Information Station in the south to the bridge at County Line Road, where the trail switches from the east side of the creek to the west. To drive to this point go north on Federal Highway

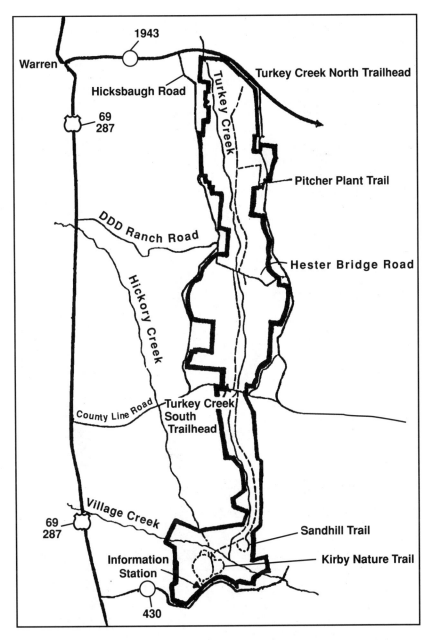

Turkey Creek Unit's Fifteen-Mile Trail

Big Cypress along Village Creek

69 from its juncture with FM 410 to its intersection with County Line Road (4.1 miles) and turn right. You can't miss the turn, sentineled as it is by V.O.'s Friendly Tavern. The Turkey Creek Trail is 3.7 miles east of this consoling mark of human kindness.

The trail head has gravel parking, a john, and two picnic tables with grills. The hike to the next bridge (the second segment in the trail) is three miles. The trail here keeps away from the creek, winding underneath loblolly pine, American holly, beech, sweetgum, and half a dozen kinds of oaks. There are more dogwood trees in this stretch than on any other trail that I have seen in the preserve. It ought to make an especially good short hike in the spring, when the dogwoods bloom.

Between the trail and the creek I counted, in the first mile, a cypress slough and two good-sized baygalls. (One of them is crossed on the trail by an elevated walkway.) In midsummer the baygalls are dry, or at any rate no longer submerged. Here mossed root tangles rise out of black earth rich with raccoon tracks and the rootings of wild hogs and armadillos. One swamp bay magnolia here has ten small trunks rising up from a single decayed stump. Near it, in a deep humus of pine needles, stand tall loblolly pines growing from a place not more than eight or ten inches higher than the black earth. On the way back to the trail I found three different fern species. While the trail itself is wide, pleasant, and interesting, there are plenty of things to find if one gets off the trail and looks around.

The second place to break a hike on Turkey Creek is the Hester Bridge Road. To get there turn off Highway 69 at the Triple D Ranch Road and head east five miles (by my odometer). The road is sandy and the bridge is "load zoned": small, and made of creosoted wood. Unlike the bridge on County Line Road to the south, this one is overhung by hardwoods and rarely sees traffic. I was there for an hour and heard little but cicadas chirring, birds chirping, and a young squirrel scurrying down the trunk of a hardwood tree. There was one deer: a buck, who plunged into the undergrowth and vanished.

Unfortunately, there are no picnic tables or johns or refuse barrels here yet.

To get to the rest of the trail, walk across the bridge east about 100 yards. The trail head is well-marked. From here to the north end of the unit is a six-mile hike. About three miles ahead the path is joined by the Pitcher Plant Trail. You can, if you wish, break off the hike there.

Turkey Creek Again: Kirby Nature and Sandhill Trails

The Kirby Nature Trail and the newer Sandhill Trail are both in the southeastern segment of the Turkey Creek Unit. That is nearly all they have in common. To hike the Kirby Trail is to enter into the swamps of South Louisiana; to hike the Sandhill Trail is almost to enter, and then abruptly leave, West Texas.

Both trails are easy to find. Take FM 420 east of highway 69, 3.7 miles to the Preserve Information Center, a log cabin set back in the shade of big hardwoods with a retinue of picnic tables and benches around it and toilets off to the side. The Kirby Nature Trail, which forms the first part of the fifteen mile long Turkey Creek Trail, starts off from this clearing.

There are two options on the Kirby Trail: an outside loop of two and one-half miles (a little more if one takes the add-on three-tenths of a mile Cypress Loop) and an inside loop of one and three-fourths miles. The main difference between the two is their length; the terrain covered is closely similar.

The Information Center does not seem to be on high ground. The minute one enters the path, however, the land begins slowly to drop off under dark shade. Some of the trees are marked: American beech (*Fagus grandifolia*), sweetgum (*Liquidambar styracifolia*), southern magnolia,(*Magnolia grandiflora*), American holly (*Ilex opaca*). There are knotted roots in

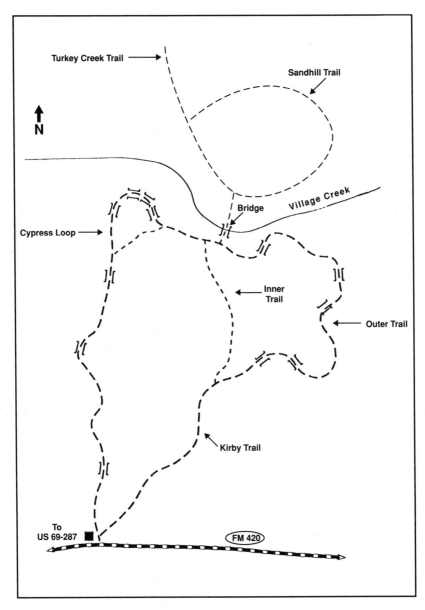

Kirby Nature Trail and Sandhill Trail

the path, scattered in a deep humus of magnolia and sweetgum leaves.

At the foot of gradual decline, the landscape and the forest change. An elevated wooden walkway traverses a swamp-baygall dominated by swamp bay magnolia (*Magnolia virginiana*) and water tupelo (*Nyssa aquatica*). I count three different species of fern here, and note the existence of an occasional titi (*Cyrilla racimiflora*) and hop hornbeam (*Ostrya virginiana*). The next swampy area—not as deep or as wet—contains loblolly pine, water oak, and a young southern magnolia. The path next passes over a fern valley along a meandering tea-colored creek with mossed green cypress knees standing sentinel.

The trail continues much the same, alternating between elevated walkways and sandy paths, swamp, semiswamp, and lowland forest. There are several bald cypress swamps, the best developed of which are found on the cypress loop. Here the water is deep, and rarely or never dries out. Some of these cypress are ancient: ten feet across at the water line, over seventy feet high, with cypress knees five and six feet tall protruding from dark, almost black water.

On the outside loop, I heard a pileated woodpecker, close kin to the extinct ivory-bill, and saw over twenty squirrels. At least three big animals crashed off through the brush—probably, but not necessarily, deer. And in every slough, swamp or baygall, something out of sight made the water undulate or made a wake just under the surface.

I had the strong feeling that I would have to hike the trail at dawn, at sundown, or on a bright moonlit night to actually see some of these creatures. Not a bad idea.

To get to the Sandhill Trail, take the big metal bridge across Village Creek where outside and inside loops converge. (You can't miss it; it's at the only large clearing on the trail.) The path here (often called the Bottomland Trail by Park Service personnel) winds across lowlands thick with vine-tangled hardwoods, black-brown cypress sloughs, beech on high loamy banks, cypress in standing water.

Pitcher Plant Bog

Several hundred yards later the path comes to an elevated metal bridge over Turkey Creek. On the other side of the bridge a cut bank rises around twenty-five feet; behind it the land rises another five or ten feet in thick woods. A left turn here puts you on the Turkey Creek Trail, a right turn leads to the Sandhill Trail, a three-fourths of a mile loop across radically different terrain: a mile, if one includes the distance from its re-juncture with Turkey Creek Trail south to the bridge.

It is surprising that an area with fifty-five inches of rain per year should produce dry landscapes. But here, as on the Arid Sandland Area farther down Village Creek, elevation and sandy soils quickly drain off rainwater, making space for dryland species. At first, this is not obvious. The trail starts in the shade of a mixed pine-hardwood forest. Soon, however, there are post oaks, shortleaf pines, then fire-tolerant longleaf pines. The wind scarcely reaches into the bottomlands; here it reaches down to the dry earth, scattering pine needles and tousling sparse grass. There are bluejack oak, and prickly pear cactus, and yucca. And trailing catchfly (*Amsonia glaberrima*), an endangered flower species.

Dry pine needles crackle underfoot. Longleaf pines no more than twenty-five or thirty-five feet tall provide minimal shade. One quickly gets a high, dry, sunbleached feeling. When the trail finally meanders back into the shade of mixed hardwoods, you have a strange sensation. How did you move suddenly from a half-forested duneland into a temperate forest? It can be hard on your sense of reality.

Last Stop at Turkey Creek: The Pitcher Plant Trail

The Pitcher Plant Trail is at the far northeast corner of the Turkey Creek Unit. To get there take FM 1943 to four miles east of Warren (off Highways 69/287) or eleven miles west of the metropolis of Fred. Turn south at the highway sign signaling the trail and continue a short distance. Parking is on the right. So are a john, and a box containing trail maps plus information.

Like the Sundew Trail, this path is blacktopped, fine for both wheelchair and walking. The first hundred yards are under pine and hardwood shade, interspersed with occasional southern magnolia saplings. The trail then becomes an elevated walkway over a pitcher plant savannah.

In the middle of the savannah the walkway intersects a large, fenced platform containing two rows of benches and several plaques explaining savannah vegetation and the character of *Sarracenia*, the pitcher plant.

I have always been fascinated by insect-eating plants— long before anyone thought up "Little Shop of Horrors." They seem so incredibly primitive—like life hesitating between plant and animal forms, unable to decide. In fact, they are a late evolutionary development, an odd reconvergence of plants towards animality, forced—or made possible—by a context of nitrogen-poor soils. The pitcher plant gives off a scent which attracts insects and lures them into its steep inner well. Insects which do not escape fall into digestive juices at the bottom of the well and are consumed. Interestingly, the pitcher plant manages to support, rather than consume, some creatures. The green lynx spider, the flesh fly, and the exyra moth survive by eating insects attracted to *Sarracenia*. There is even a mosquito whose larvae survive in the plant's digestive juices.

Many other interesting plants live in this area besides *Sarracenia*. Ferns, orchids, many species of wildflowers, and other insectivores thrive there in season.

[133]

The Pitcher Plant Trail is not a loop. It continues over the pitcher plant bog and descends from its wooden walkway into a forest of young pines and then of dogwood, white oak, and post oak. Not long afterwards it joins the Turkey Creek Trail, which runs north and south fifteen miles through the length of the Turkey Creek Unit.

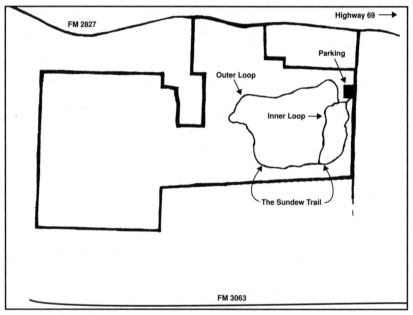

Hickory Creek Savannah Unit's Sundew Trail

Hickory Creek Savannah Unit: The Sundew Trail

The Hickory Creek Savannah, at 703 acres, seems almost too small to be a unit. It contains, however, almost perfect examples of both longleaf pine uplands and pine savannah wetlands, with transition communities in between. And it con-tains one of the best short trail systems in the Preserve: the Sundew Trail.

To get to the Hickory Creek Savannah turn west on FM 2827 off Federal Highway 69 (not far north from the turnoff for the Preserve Visitor's Information Center near Turkey Creek). Turn left again two-tenths of a mile later (now you're headed south) and soon, on the right, you will see a sign marked Sundew Trail. There's a good-sized parking lot, partly shaded, and nearby, a small pavilion for picnicking. There are also rest rooms and directions for hiking.

The trail has two loops. The first, broad and blacktopped, runs a quarter of a mile, and is easily traversable by wheelchair. The second "outer" loop is a mile long, and must be walked on foot.

In late June, when I visited, the soil was dry, and it would have been easy to hike the unit without getting one's feet wet. A single hard rain could change that overnight, however, flood-ing the low places and turning the high ones into loamy mud. That is why at least one-third of each trail is elevated wooden walkway. Not only do you not have to get your feet wet: even in the wettest times you can make the whole loop.

A savannah is a stressed environment. Dry and wet at the same time, it is rich in species and poor in soils. Through the decades, water draining through low areas leaches nutrients from the soil. Oxidation cements fine-grained soil particles together, creating a "hardpan" which holds water: as if the area were underlain by a sheet of metal, impervious to rain. Mean-while pine needles produce highly acidic soils. These three factors (acidic soils, low nutrient content and poor drainage) determine the kind of plants that can grow here.

Among these species are, starting from the ground up, the insect-eaters: pitcher plants (*Sarracenia*), bladderworts (*Utricula*) and sundews (*Drosera*); the snowy orchid (*Habenaria*) and the grass pink orchid (*Calopogon*); the bracken fern; sphagnum moss, colic root, meadow beauty, and pine-woods rose-gentian. Higher and larger are thickets of yaupon holly and titi, wax myrtle, and gallberry holly. Then come the trees. In time most of this area would graduate to longleaf pine. At present, stands of longleaf compete for space with black gum and sweetgum trees, with several species of red oak and post oak, shortleaf pine, even a few young southern magnolias. On the outer loop a large dogwood tree shades a picnic table and benches—a pleasant shade to sit under, especially in the spring when the dogwood blooms.

In the past, savannahs were kept free of brush and invading species by fires that regularly burned hot and fast through the dried grasses of late summer. Today the savannahs must be burned annually by the Park Service to sustain their unique mix of species. With time this procedure will result not only in sustained populations of orchids, insectivores, and related plants, but in the re-establishment of longleaf pine as the dominant tree.

Big Sandy Creek Unit: Beaver Slide Trail

There is no parking area for Beaver Slide Trail other than the shoulders of FM 943, nor are there picnic tables. The trail entrance, however, is well-marked. At the entrance a cardboard poster proclaims: "Endangered paddlefish. Important. Please release paddlefish where they are caught. Possession is against the law. Please contact your local Texas Parks and Wildlife Department Office."

The trail goes first across a typical baygall: waterstanding tupelo, chain fern, swamp bay magnolia. Beyond the baygall is an area beginning to recover from pine cutting for control (if it really does control) of the ubiquitous pine bark beetle. Then the trail rises over a tree-shaded clay dam. To the east lies a cypress pond, its far side covered with lily pads; to the west runs a shallow slough winding through dark shade. Someone has lost a plastic fishing float on a high cypress limb. A cuckoo lights on the limb, spears an insect, flies off. The cork jiggles.

The name "Beaver Slide" may seem to proclaim some sort of mammalian Wet 'n Wild. That is unfortunate. There are beaver here, and they do have "slides"—well-worn clay paths leading down three or four feet to pond water. What this trail really is, however, is a mile long loop—much of it on elevated walkways—across bottomland thick with swamps, ponds, sloughs, and creeks.

Past the dam the path deadends at the still water of an abandoned creek, and the loop begins. On its far side the loop follows the banks of Big Sandy Creek. In between one loses sight of Big Sandy, but never of water. A slight difference in elevation here can change everything. A foot higher and one has a beech grove: parklike, shady, the ground a mesh of gnarled roots and loamy sand. A foot lower and one has swamp or semiswamp, with tea-colored standing water and water-tolerant trees and shrubs.

The day I was there a group of kids from a summer camp at Woodville were stretched out eating lunch at the place where the trail deadends. They told me they thought the woods were beautiful there, and asked if I had seen a beaver or a paddlefish. The paddlefish, I explained, are an endangered species; as such they are few and far between. As for the beaver, try as the Park Service may, it's still impossible to get them to come out in the daytime to perform for tourists.

The kids were not impressed.

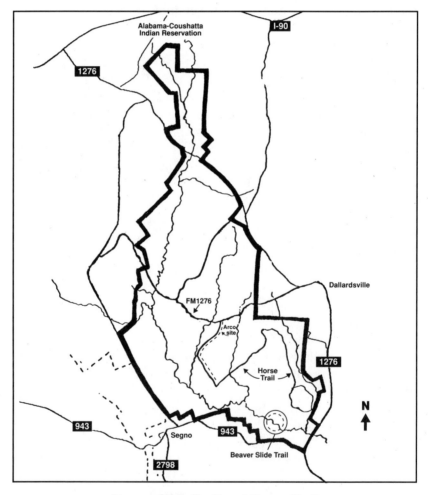

Beaver Slide Trail and Horse Trail

Big Sandy Creek Unit: The Horse Trail

The Big Sandy Horse Trail turns south 3.7 miles from downtown Dallardsville, two miles west of the cutoff from FM 1276 onto Sunflower Road. The trail head contains a big circular parking area with a tree-shaded center where horses can be tethered. It also boasts a john, three picnic tables and two grills, and even, over to the side, two wooden hitching posts. Anyone who wants to ride horseback here may do so without a permit; off-trail horseback riding, however, is forbidden. The trail is nine miles long (an eighteen mile round trip). Besides being maintained for horseback riding, it is open for hiking and all-terrain bicycling.

At 320+ feet above sea level, the Big Sandy Unit contains easily the highest point in the preserve. (Compare this with the Beaumont Unit, whose southern heights rise to five feet.) The horse trail begins in an upland dominated by shortleaf pine punctuated by oak, sweetgum, and hickory. Black cherry, yaupon, and dogwood make up the understory. As the trail descends, the woods shift towards a beech-loblolly-magnolia association. The transition, however, is not continuous. Every patch of woods here seems older or younger than every other, creating an odd unevenness. Even so, these woods are, as a rule, tall and lush.

About a mile down the trail, on the left, there is a recent eleven-acre Arco drilling site. The drilling there produced no oil, but it did create a barren rectangle. Around the perimeter pines are beginning to grow; towards the center grasses and a few wildflowers are beginning to cover sandy clay.

Two and a half miles down the trail where it turns abruptly to the northeast, there is a "beaver pond" several hundred yards wide, quite unusual in this upland country. I was struck by the fact that the pond is not on any of the old "topo" maps of the area. Most of the bald cypress are young, possibly fifteen to twenty years old. The water is clean, and surprisingly clear. Back in the swamp stands a single cypress patriarch at least four feet in diameter. A cypress that massive would ordinarily tower eighty or ninety feet above its surroundings. The top is missing from this one, but it is still up at around sixty feet. It was probably struck by lightning.

Except for the old patriarch, this has all the markings of a new swamp, and it is. The enforcement of trapping controls have allowed the beaver to return to the Big Sandy Unit and build dams downslope near the creek. It is in this new water that the young cypress and rushes and hollies now grow. This area was probably a beaver pond when the first European saw it. It has returned to the same state. If the old fire-topped cypress could speak, it would doubtless explain that this was exactly how God had intended things. And it would point to its dozens of new sons and daughters now digging their roots into wet, sandy loam as perfect verification of its opinion.

Past the beaver pond, less than 1000 yards to the northeast, the trail crosses Simon's Branch. Flooding and storm winds here have toppled many trees by the bridge. Even so, I found it worthwhile to wander up and down the creek under its remaining beech and pines. Small bass swam in its tea-colored pools. Ferns hung from its steep banks.

The loop at the end of the Horse Trail is in the far southeastern corner of the unit, at one point almost touching its fence line. It is not far from Beaver Slide Trail, and from the map looks as if it should be down in the lowlands. Not so. Most of the trail "heads the creeks," keeping to the high ground, usually along the crests of the ridges. The final loop circles a hill which looks down at the creek bottom, fifty to sixty feet below. This is scarcely a mountain view, but it makes a nice contrast with the low flat country to the south.

Big Sandy Creek Unit: The Woodlands Trail

The Woodlands Trail is in the Big Sandy Unit, on FM 1276 just three and a half miles south of Highway 190 (five and a half miles north of Dallardsville).

Woodlands Trail is a good name, though it is not inclusive. Not only are there "woods" here; there are swamps, sloughs, baygalls, several different sorts of creeks, and also meadows, canebreaks, old fence lines, and a low pine-magnolia ridge. And, at the beginning, a pond.

The pond, created by a rancher many years ago, is something less than an acre in size, and is now grown up around its margins with willow, pine, sweetgum and brush. The water is clear, fish are visible jumping among the water weeds, a trail circuits the pond, and there are four or five places where one can cast in a lure—more, if one is acrobatic.

The trail starts on a dry upland among shortleaf pine, and drops off slowly into older, thicker shade. The hill slopes become more open and parklike under hardwoods as one descends. At least they do until one reaches the bottomland tangle, where the path turns into an elevated walkway over a tupelo slough.

Besides sloughs, swamps, and winding creeks there are occasional stands of cane. Early travelers in Texas often wrote of canebrakes miles in length and higher than a person on horseback. Impenetrable and pathless, they were the haunts of bear and panther. They were also soon to be victims of civilization: easily burned in dry times and grazed down happily by cattle, who sought out the tender young shoots.

Removal of livestock—which regularly graze the piney woods—has led to the regrowth of stands of cane like these on the Woodlands Trail. Conceivably they will once again take over large areas of the bottomland.

It is nearly impossible to capture on paper the diversity along this trail. Some of the trees are ancient: my favorite is a massive sweetgum three feet in diameter climbed by a vine as big around as my leg; next in line is a good-sized native pecan spreading like a live oak, fifty-five feet high by my estimate and eighty feet across. Any tree that sprawls like that did not grow up in a forest; it grew up in a field, by itself, where there was room to spread.

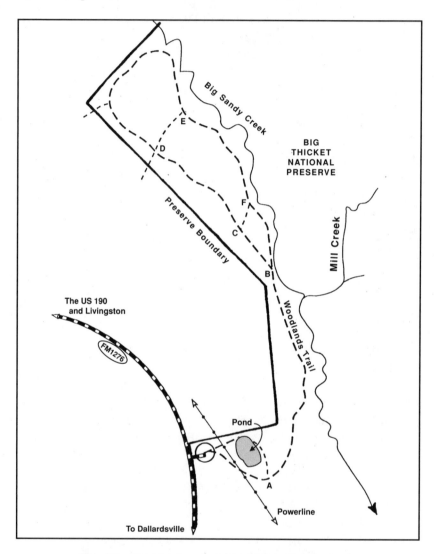

The Big Sandy Creek Unit's Woodlands Trail

Sure enough, not far from it one comes out into a meadow-land, where a grassy path meanders among blackberry thickets.

The entire trail is 5.4 miles long, longer than many will want. One can cut this distance, however, by taking cross-paths across the long loop that makes up most of the distance. There are two of these shortcuts, the first of which trims the journey down to just over three miles, the second to around four and a half. Nothing stops you, of course, from turning back at any point.

I have to confess that for my tastes the last part of the trail is the best, and worth the effort. Part of an old Carter Lumber Company path, it is the most primitive, world-lost, vine-tangled part of the trail. Many years ago an alligator escaped from its pen not far upstream in the Alabama-Coushatta Indian Reservation. By now eight to ten feet long, it ranges along this part of Big Sandy creek, occasionally seen by Park Service rangers, who never stop it to ask any questions.

Alligators, incidentally, rarely—if ever—attack human beings. They tend, like most creatures, to go their own way.

Beech Creek Unit: The Beech Woods Trail

The Beech Creek Unit was infested with pine bark beetles in the mid-1970s, before the National Park Service could purchase and take possession of it. Of its 5089 acres, around 1200 (one-fifth) were destroyed by the Texas Forest Service in a botched attempt to control the beetle and to harvest still-usable pine timber. (The Texas Forest Service is an agency of state government affiliated with Texas A & M University.) Most of the damage was done in the unit's southwest portion. One might protest that in cutting pines in a mixed pine-hardwood forest

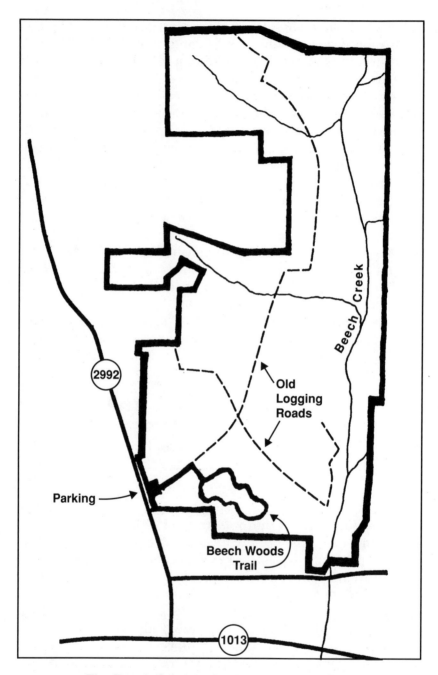

The Beech Creek Unit's Beech Woods Trail

one can only do minimal damage. Unfortunately, falling pines destroy hardwood timber; so do bulldozers and "skidders." Woods which have been treated for pine beetles often look as if they have been bombed and strafed.

The result of this systematic mistreatment is that the National Park Service has declared much of this unit "off limits." Trails will not be put into these areas for decades, until the forest recovers. The only trail presently in the unit (the Beech Woods Trail) is a mile-long loop in its southern end.

To get there turn east off Highway 69 at Hillister onto FM 1013, then go east 10.6 miles to FM 2992. Drive north 1.5 miles; the trail—with three picnic tables, a john, and plenty of parking—is on the right.

Starting out on an old logging road, the Beech Woods Trail turns off three-tenths of a mile later onto a loop. The forest floor here is uneven and sandy between leaf carpet. Everywhere one looks there are hammocks, downslopes, drainage patterns. Here beech predominate, interspersed with magnolias and American holly. There are few pines; most were harvested in the 1930s.

These are not the dramatically large beech of the northern part of the unit. They are moderate-sized, though their shade creates a typical open, park-like expanse. There are two elevated walkways here, over sandy baygalls thick with sphagnum moss. It's a nice walk through a pleasant beechwood ecosystem, a vision of what much of the upper Big Thicket once was like, mile after mile.

There is a second set of trails in this unit: two lumber company roads which intersect, one heading southeast and halting before nearly reaching Beech Creek, the other running all the way to the north end of the unit. The Park Service has no plans to maintain these roads, but for the present, at least, they are hikeable. A trek on either soon brings one to the site of pine beetle "control." The results are interesting. After a decade and a half, young pines have regrown twenty to twenty-five feet high. They are packed close together, their lower branches shaggy with brown fallen needles. Some are already beginning to die, failing in the competition for sunlight. Beneath them, in dense shade, various saplings (oaks, sweetgum, maple, holly) are beginning to emerge. Given time—two decades?—this will be moving from a pine to a mixed pine-hardwood forest. Given more time, beech and magnolia will begin to dominate, reestablishing the ancient forest association.

This is one of the hopeful facts about nature: its tendency to heal and reassert itself, whether in a skin cut, a harsh illness, or a pine beetle "control." Looking at the green wreckage of the Beech Creek Unit, however, makes one only sadly optimistic. Nature's capacity to reachieve its norms is limited, and takes place slowly. In places like Beech Creek—in spite of their unusually fast rate of recuperation—it will be our grandchildren, not us, who will be able to observe what our grandparents could easily see here, and probably took for granted.

Actually, the description of this forest is partly inaccurate. Some pines and hardwoods did manage to survive the Texas Forest Service juggernaut. Where they did survive, they are regal. Isolated loblollies and beech and water oak soar above this forest. They—the old-timers—are massive among struggling saplings.

A word about primitive hiking here. The best of it is in the northern third of the unit, and there, because of land ownership patterns, access from the highway (FM 1746) is difficult. In the southern part of the unit, Beech Creek is more a blackwater cypress tupelo slough than a temperate forest creek. The beech and magnolia forest there grow on slopes a hundred feet away from the creek. One has to get farther north, where the high, sloping banks close in on the creek, to see, really, what this unit was created for.

One more note:

In 1976 a bear was discovered along Beech Creek. It was a yearling, and probably would not have weighed much more than a hundred pounds. It had been shot in the head with a .22 rifle and, apparently, had wandered back along the creek to die. Its skull found its way into the archives of the Cornell University Department of Biology. The rest of the skeleton was taken to the Big Thicket Museum at Saratoga, where it was placed in a box marked: "Can Anyone Reassemble this Bear?" To date there have been no takers.

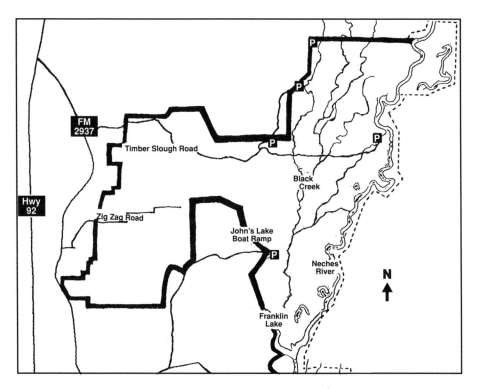

Neches River Corridor's Jack Gore Baygall Unit

Neches River Corridor: Canoe Trips Medium and Long

In 1964, when conservationists set out for the second time to save what was left of the Big Thicket, not even a handful considered including the Neches River in a park or monument. Emphasis fell on what is now the Lance Rosier Unit and the Pine Island Bayou watershed. The emphasis gradually shifted, however, not so much to take in the river as include the entire diversity of the Thicket region. If this truly was the Biological Crossroads of North America, as Thicket protagonists insisted, then the end result of efforts to conserve it—or at least a fragment of it—would have to mirror all of its diversity, or as much as acreage would allow.

The earliest proposals for a park—the so-called "String of Pearls" suggested by the National Park Service, largely with the blessings of lumber interests—contained two units on the Neches: the Neches Bottom Unit and the Beaumont Unit. The Beaumont Unit, at the confluence of Pine Island Bayou and the Neches, seemed only an extension of the effort to protect the bayou with its wilderness of palmetto thickets and cypress sloughs. The Neches Bottom Unit, though it did not fit this picture, was a virtually untouched bottomland forest with a wealth of heron and ibis rookeries and immense trees. The inclusion of the Jack Gore Baygall Unit later, added still another ecosystem to the Thicket Park, and a third to the Neches River system. It also created several miles of protected river corridor.

If the primary goal of Big Thicket conservation was to preserve diversity, that goal soon led to a second: connection. A park could not hope to survive as an aggregate of unconnected units. That had been the objection to the "string of pearls": not only was it made up of very small pearls, but the pearls were also without a string. Gradually conservationists came around to the idea that the Neches River Units would have to be strung together by a corridor protecting both sides of the river. They may have wanted, badly, to use that scarce acreage elsewhere; but its use on the river seemed increasingly inescapable.

The result was the virtual creation of a National Wild and Scenic River, stretching from B. A. Steinhagen Lake at the juncture of the Neches and the Angelina Rivers on the north, south to the Beaumont City Limits: ninety-three miles as the crow flies.

The Neches River is scenic, and is rich with bird, fish, reptile and mammal life. Stretches of the river are so world-lost and remote that one can, while canoeing, actually believe that one has lost touch with cities and suburbs forever. But it is nowhere a "white water" stream. If that is what one means by wild, it is not "wild." The goal is not to pit one's will and skill against an overwhelming torrent, but to explore and reflect; and to allow nature to percolate through one's nerve endings.

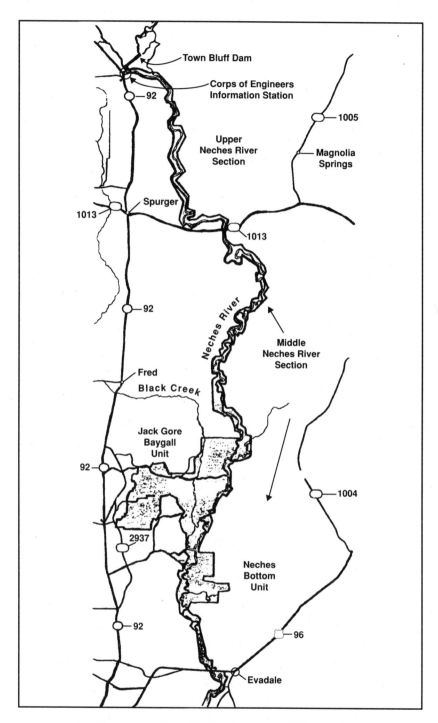

The Neches River Corridor's Upper and Middle Sections

Geologically the Neches River Corridor divides into three sections: an upper region, where the river still cuts into high, wooded banks and waters run fast; a middle region where the banks begin to subside and the river begins to deposit its sediments; and a lower section, flatter, more alluvial, very nearly bluff-to-bluff swamp. The ecology here follows the geology, with the lower section rich in water-tolerant wetland species and the upper section in species adapted to hammocks and hillslopes. The middle section, predictably, is a patchwork of all of these.

It would be nice if the highway bridges and nearby settlements on the Neches followed this threefold pattern, but they do not. Without exception, prescriptions for Neches float trips are not three-fold, but four-fold. Each begins with a bridge or community, where one can get a canoe or a skiff into the river and a community or a bridge where one can get them out. The first float begins below Dam B and ends at the FM 1013 bridge. The second begins at this bridge and ends at U. S. Highway 96. The third begins here and continues down to the Lakeview Community on the east side of the river, with a road out to FM 1131. The fourth begins at the Lakeview Community and ends at the Beaumont Country Club, where there is a boat ramp.

Each float trip is different. From Highway 96 south, river traffic increases. The nearer one is to Beaumont, the more boats one encounters. South of the Lakeview takeout and particularly on weekends, one is likely to find that scourge of canoers, skiffers, and rowers: the water skier, plus the drunk on the twenty-thousand dollar boat. The farther south one gets, also, the harder it is to find a camping spot on a bank. On the third float there are only sandbars, unless there is high water.

In all of this area there is plenty to see—at least if one is willing to explore. Using the land acquisition maps of the Park Service, I count sixty-two bodies of water partly or entirely inside the Preserve Corridor between Dam B and Beaumont, besides the river. These are of almost every conceivable kind, as their names suggest: Walnut Run, Gourd Vine Eddy, Burnt Slough, Black Water Slough, Wheeler Cutoff Lake, Clear Lake, Shade Lake, Alligator Lake, Massey Lake Slough, Sandy Lake.

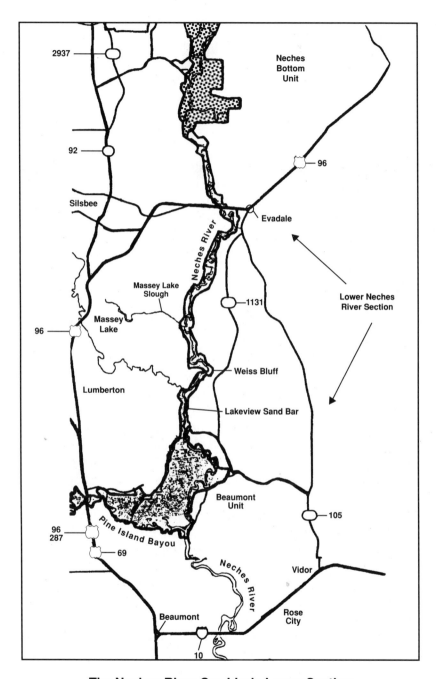

The Neches River Corridor's Lower Section

Some are no bigger than a suburban lot, others are as wide as the Neches and several miles long. The joy of floating this river is *not* to try to reach each mile-post as quickly as possible—for that, try the Interstate. It is to paddle or trek one's way into places where people are seldom likely to go, to find the unsuspected heron or spoonbill or stork rookery, or the bald eagle perched on a high dead limb, or the signs of river otter on a sandbar or in a clay bank. It is to see a huge alligator gar basking in the sandy shallows of a cutoff slough, or a deer come down watchfully to the edge of a darkwater pond at sunrise.

The float from Dam B to FM 1013 runs fourteen crow-flight miles and takes four-and-a-half to six hours, if one stops neither to camp nor to explore. There are two places to put in: a boat ramp at the end of a blacktop road running east from the juncture of FM 92 and FM 1746 (small fee for launching) and, on the east side, from Jasper on County Road 777 through East End Park of the U. S. Corps of Engineers (no fee). Both the Corps of Engineers and Texas State Parks and Wildlife provide camping on Steinhagen Lake.

During the first four or five miles here there are several permanent residences within view of the river. The last several miles, however, are isolated. There are high sandstone and iron ore bluffs, numerous sandbars and a variety of vegetation types. Due to the proximity of private lands, the Park Service recommends camping on sandbars and allows it only by permit. Any preserve ranger station has permits, and they are free.

Scaly-barked river birches, sweetgum, pine, and big white-barked sycamores dominate the river banks, screening out wildlife sightings and often limiting visibility to the river corridor itself. There are plenty of wading birds: great egret, cattle egret, and great blue heron among them.

The take-out boat ramp is just above the bridge on FM 1013, on the west side. From the ramp to a parking area is 100 feet, and requires hand-carrying a canoe or other boat.

From FM 1013 to U.S. Highway 96 is forty miles—twenty straight hours of canoeing. It seems fair to say that this is not a one-day, but at least a two-day trip. Just below the FM 1013 bridge on the east bank there is a private boat ramp (small fee required), making boat access easy.

Most of those who have made the trip suggest breaking it at the Hardin County Park at Timber Slough Road, where there is—in dry weather—primitive camping. For the first twenty-five miles (five miles below the Hardin County Park) there are large sand bars which make good campsites. From there on, finding camping space becomes harder, with some small sand bars and a few high banks providing opportunities.

As noted above, midway through this trip the character of the Neches changes. Above the Hardin County Park it is still cutting its high banks and depositing sandbars on the inside of its curves. Below the park the river begins to deposit more earth than it cuts. The result is low, flat, sometimes swampy banks and the complete absence of bluffs. There are more oxbow lakes and backwater cypress sloughs. Those looking for an experience of primeval solitude can—to cite only one possibility—find it on a side trip up Deep Slough, about six-and-a-half miles north of Highway 96 on the east side of the river.

The lower part of this float is, and will remain, the most remote segment of the river, partly because of the creek-laced, swampy nature of the terrain but also because of the presence of the Jack Gore Baygall and Neches Bottom Units. These areas are presently without hiking trails—at best one finds the fading remains of old lumber company roads. (The exception is the Timber Slough Road.) These areas repay the effort to explore them, however. I'm thinking not only of the root tangles and clear springs of the baygalls, but of a stand of sweetgum in the Neches Bottom Unit so huge that standing by one of them is like standing near a wall, not a tree.

Take-out is just south of the Highway 96 bridge on the west side of the river. This is a "semi-improved" boat ramp: good in dry weather, but less good in wet. True monsoon renders the road to it impassable.

The third float trip, from U.S. Highway 96 to the Lakeview community, runs sixteen miles and requires approximately eight hours. In one respect it is wilder and less "humanized" than the first float, south of Dam B. The low, stream-rich

Spring day on Village Creek

landscape contains innumerable creeks, sloughs, backwaters, and semiswamps leading off the river, each rich in vegetation and wildlife. At the same time (after all, one is getting near Beaumont) there are more cabins and other human intrusions within view—including a small airport. Camping is largely limited to sandbars in this section, due to the low, marshy character of the riverbank.

Input here is just below the river bridge on Highway 96 on the west side of the river. Take-out is at a privately improved boat ramp on a bayou near the Lakeview Community (on the east bank).

The final float trip on the Neches runs from Lakeview Community to Beaumont—in fact, to the Beaumont Country Club. This makes a good morning or afternoon trip, requiring around five hours' canoe time. Only a few small areas are high and dry enough here to afford camping space, and these are submerged in high water. This trip is, for most practical purposes, for canoeing only. There are plenty of side trips. Near Beaumont, Scatterman Lake off the west bank and Bunn's Lake off the east make interesting circuits, with their jungle islands and cypress-lined banks.

The take-out is not actually *in*, but closely adjacent to, the Beaumont Country Club. Do not ask the alligators here for Grey Poupon. They get terribly irritated.

Rather than heading directly to Beaumont there is an alternative float trip from the Lakeview community south. Almost directly across the Neches from Lakeview begins the Lower Neches River Valley Canal, which forms the northwest border of the Beaumont Unit. At its juncture with Pine Island Bayou the canal goes underground (in huge pipes) and emerges on the other side. It's a strict no-no to go through the pipes. A brief portage here affords a float down the bayou to the Neches River. Unless the river is high it is not hard to paddle eight miles up the river to Lakeview, completing a sixteen-mile round trip. If the river is high, pull out at the ramp at the country club. Remember what I said about the alligators.

This description scarcely does justice either to the Neches River or to the different float trips. A couple more points are in order.

The first is that the Park Service provides maps of the river describing both interesting natural features and nearby roads and settlements. Park Service maps also depict "river miles": miles from the input at Dam B to the out-take at Beaumont, much as Interstate maps provide "highway miles." The Park Service also marks these miles in the river with large, highly visible wood paddles. One can then compare one's place on the map with one's actual place on the river: useful in planning camping and side trips, and even more useful for knowing one is not lost.

The second point is that there is or will soon be a pamphlet written by Howard Peacock for the National Park Service describing the Neches and other parts of the preserve in greater detail than is attempted here. One might want to know some-

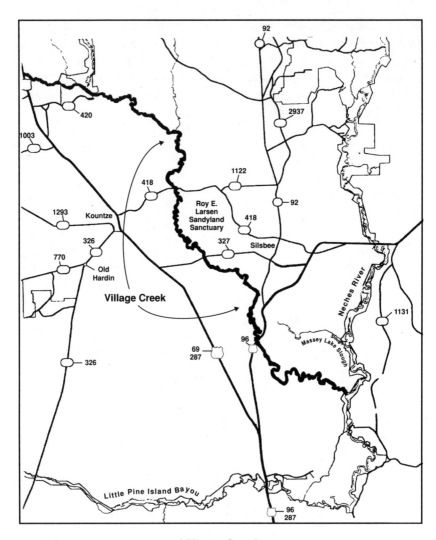

Village Creek

thing about Bearman's Bluff and how it was named, or about the two (still unexplored) Indian mounds between Weiss' Bluff and Cook's Lake. Or one might want to know more about which side trips are interesting, or even about former river pirates on the Neches. A little searching should turn up more detailed accounts of the river, and make for an even more interesting trip.

Village Creek

Big Sandy Creek and Village Creek are the same stream divided by two names. To the north and west it is called Big Sandy. To the south and east of Highway 69/287 it is called Village Creek. Big Sandy (named for its banks and sandy water) is really not big. It could be canoed in high water, if the canoer were somewhat acrobatic and willing to dodge snags, limbs, and fallen trees. Village Creek (named for a now vanished Indian village) is a more likely canoeing stream. It is twenty to thirty feet wide—less in dry periods but almost always canoeable. Occasionally it will flow through cypress swamps, more often through pine and hardwood forests. As is true of the Neches, hills, bluffs, and high cut banks are more likely on its upper than lower reaches.

Like the Neches, Village Creek is by no stretch of imagination a whitewater stream. In my experience the best name for it is—unless one is portaging around an occasional fallen tree—idyllic. Forest overhang shades much of the way, sometimes forming a closed canopy over mildly tea-colored water. Wading birds of all kinds stalk along the banks, flying away with shrill cries when surprised. Smaller warblers, cuckoos, cardinals, jays, doves, and nut hatches forage and nest in the shady overhang. The deep woods shadows are broken by the dazzle of white sandbars: looking like snowdrifts under the noon sun.

From Highway 69 to the Neches River on Village Creek is thirty-seven miles. That is a several day float trip, complicated by the fact that there is no "take-out" place at the confluence of the creek and the Neches River. (You have to go a bit south, to the Lakeview Community, to rescue your boat.) Luckily, there are any number of places along the creek to put in and take out a canoe. The first is at FM 420, one mile downstream from Turkey Creek and six creek miles from Highway 69. The next is at FM 418 east of Kountze, fourteen miles downstream from FM 420, and the next is eight miles later at State Highway 327, east of Silsbee. Nine miles downstream there is a Texas State Parks and Wildlife boat ramp at U.S. Highway 96. About six miles further on, Village Creek flows into the Neches.

There are, obviously, a lot of ways to canoe Village Creek, long and short. Each will have his or her own preference. Mine is the eight miles from FM 418 south to State Highway 327. The put-ins and take-outs are handy in almost any weather, and the time is less than a day. Speed merchants can make it in one morning, but that is for racing. The entire float runs through the Larsen Sanctuary on the east and land leased by the Nature Conservancy from Temple-Inland on the west. There is time to relax and watch the birds, or the weather, or to hike out across the Larsen Sanctuary and look for Alligator Grass Lake or just enjoy the arid sandlands. There is time to paddle up Cypress Creek from its union with Village Creek. (I never go there without seeing at least five species of wading birds.) Nature is like a book. The sandland float trip makes it easy to read.

A word of caution: as this is being written, most of the Village Creek Corridor is privately owned, either by timber interests or individual landholders. The only places where overnight camping is allowed are the Turkey Creek Unit, the Larsen Sanctuary, and the Village Creek State Park. For that, one has to get a permit from the National Park Service, Nature Conservancy, or Texas State Parks and Wildlife, respectively.

Roy E. Larsen Sandyland Sanctuary

The Roy E. Larsen Sandyland Sanctuary was donated to the Nature Conservancy in 1977 by Temple-Eastex. Easy to find, its northern boundary is on FM 418 just east of Village Creek. The southern border (which contains the trail head) is on Highway 327, just two-and-a-half miles west of Silsbee.

Created to protect a unique arid sandland (or sandyland) plant association, the nearly 2400 acres of the Sandyland Sanctuary are highly diverse, including baygalls, stream flood plains, and wetland pine habitat. Throughout its length the sanctuary fronts on Village Creek, affording some nice views from the bluffs and a pleasant, especially convenient two-thirds of a day float trip from the north end of the sanctuary to the south. (See the section on Canoe trips.)

There are three trails, which intersect and have segments in common. The Interpretive Trail (.8 mile), both the shortest and the most informative, winds through beech-magnolia, arid sandland, baygall, and sandland associations. There are fifteen "stops" on this trail. A list available at the registration area details natural features near each of these stops, from leaf-cutter ants to wildflowers to tree species.

The Flood Plain Trail (2.8 miles) loops through the lowlands along Village Creek into a frequently flooded closed canopy hardwood forest. Bald cypress and water tupelo dominate sloughs and overflow channels here; beech, magnolia, and white oak flourish on stream terraces and "transition slopes" (the hills up from the creek).

The longest hike (four miles) is called the Succession Pond Trail. Most of it meanders across arid sandland reminiscent of the Sand Hill Trail in the Turkey Creek Unit. As on the much briefer Sand Hill Trail, one finds a dry, open woodland of longleaf pines and scrub oaks. This is an especially interesting place to look for wildflowers, including three endangered species: white firewheel, Texas trailing phlox, and scarlet catchfly.

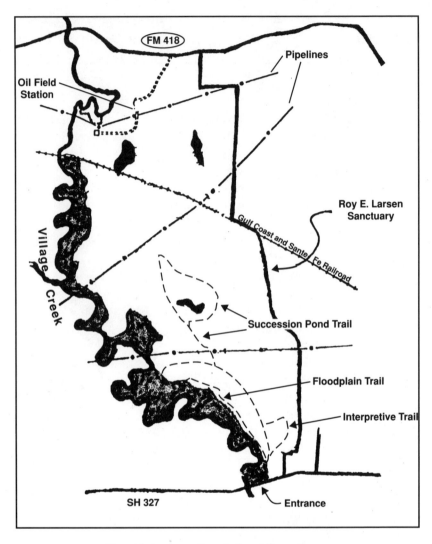

Roy E. Larsen Sandyland Sanctuary

While not wishing to belittle these, I have to confess my soaring preference for a feature which Nature Conservancy maps merely term "succession pond." Its maiden name is Alligator Grass Lake, and it has at least three things going for it. There are alligators here, though efforts to make them come out and dance for tourists, I hear, have produced nothing but gnashing of teeth and otherwise surly behavior. I have never seen them. The second unusual feature is the pond's false bottom, a sheet of decaying vegetation about seven feet down from the surface at the center, formed by moss and sinking grass, leaves, and water weed. A pole thrust through this apparent bed enters another six or seven feet of clear water before finally reaching the real floor.

Finally, there are floating islands of vegetation on Alligator Grass Lake: big enough to support grass, flowers, brush, and even small bushes. These are nowhere tied down. On a day with a strong south wind they will be on the northern end of the pond. A north wind pushes them to the southern end.

The Larsen Sanctuary is not part of the Big Thicket National Preserve. It belongs to Nature Conservancy, a private nonprofit organization with some 1200 similar preserves nationally. Since June, 1980, trails here have been open to the public during daylight hours. Those who want to get a guided tour or to bring a large group, be sure to contact the sanctuary manager [(409) 385-4135, or P.O. Box 909, Silsbee, TX 77656].

Village Creek State Park

Texas State Parks and Wildlife purchased this site for Village Creek State Park in late 1979. As I am writing, "development" of the park is finally in motion. By most accounts it should be open for vacationers by spring or summer, 1993. That this has taken fourteen years is a tribute to the perverse way in which time moves in the Big Thicket: quickly for clearcutting, glacially for conservation and recreation.

One of the reasons for the wait was fiscal: Texas Parks and Wildlife was short on funds for developing new parks. Another was less predictable. Not long after purchase of the nearly thousand-acre site, heavy rains sent Village Creek surging over much of its acreage. It had been a long time since there had been a flood that high, and for a while bureaucrats in Austin considered selling the site. How, they asked, can you build campsites and cabins if you know that sooner or later—possibly sooner— they are going to be washed away? Then, in a move that will make their reputation for all time, the parks and wildlife folk hit upon a solution. Why not develop the high places and leave the lowlands relatively undeveloped?

And that is how Village Creek State Park, with its two mile creek frontage, is being put together. It had been understood since the beginning that state parks in the Thicket would provide canoe and boat launches, cabins, playgrounds, trailer dumps and hookups, and the group facilities that the national preserve would not. Easy access to the creek will be provided, along with a boat ramp, a fish cleaning facility, johns and garbage pick-up. All this for a minimal fee.

In the dark, forgettable past, Texas Parks and Wildlife had a bad reputation for mistreating the acreage under its control. (The worst case was a projected golf course, which would have destroyed hill country habitat of the rare golden-cheeked warbler.) This, I believe, is no longer true. The personnel involved in establishing Village Creek State Park are as concerned as any

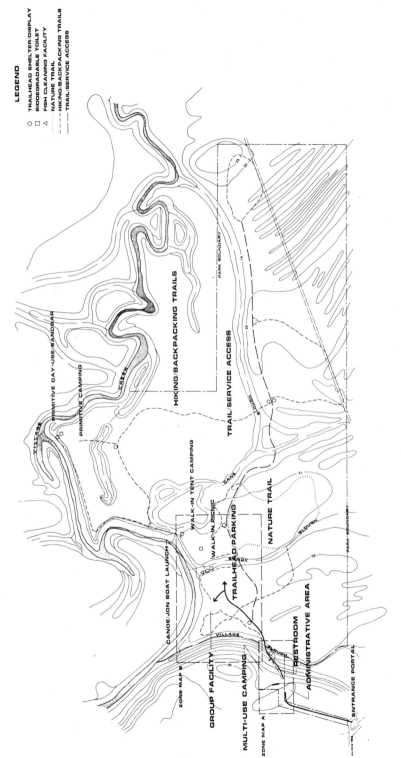

Village Creek State Park

LEGEND

○   TRAILHEAD SHELTER/DISPLAY
□   BIODEGRADABLE TOILET
△   FISH CLEANING FACILITY
      NATURE TRAIL
- - - HIKING/BACKPACKING TRAILS
— — TRAIL/SERVICE ACCESS

HIKING/BACKPACKING TRAILS

TRAIL/SERVICE ACCESS

PRIMITIVE DAY-USE/SANDBAR

PRIMITIVE CAMPING

VILLAGE

CREEK

WALK-IN TENT CAMPING

WALK-IN PICNIC

CANE

NATURE TRAIL

SLOUGH

HEADLE

SANDY

CANOE/JON BOAT LAUNCH

TRAILHEAD/PARKING

ZONE MAP B

GROUP FACILITY

VILLAGE

MULTI-USE CAMPING

ZONE MAP A

RESTROOM

ADMINISTRATIVE AREA

SLOUGH

ENTRANCE PORTAL

ALMA DR.

PARK BOUNDARY

conservationist to safeguard its natural features; so were those
who planned it. Alligator slides have been seen in remote parts
of the park, as well as signs of river otter. Texas Parks and
Wildlife will make sure that these areas remain remote. Besides
tourist facilities, there will be nature trails and primitive camping. In developing this site, the parks people will leave by far the
greater part undeveloped.

It is easy to find. Take Alma Drive off old U.S. Highway 96
in Lumberton and head east. You will end up at the park
entrance. (Old Highway 96 parallels the new Highway 96, which
runs north-south through Lumberton; if you miss it, take the
next right headed east, in town.)

Two more points. Village Creek State Park is diverse.
Uplands and slope forests there contrast with meander sloughs
and cypress swamps. Nature trails through these areas will be
well worth following. Equally important is the large sandbar
along Village Creek within the park boundaries, which will
make a perfect camping place for Village Creek canoers, as well
as a "take-out" place, with access to the road.

Pine Island Bayou

The Park Service, in its printout on canoeing in the Big
Thicket, describes Pine Island Bayou from FM 770 just west of
Saratoga to U.S. Highway 69 in Beaumont as adding up to forty-
nine miles of canoe stream. That depends on the weather. I have
hiked down the bayou from FM 770 many times in dry months;
in fact, I have hiked many times *in* the bayou, with dry feet. In
dry times the upper reaches of Pine Island Bayou become a
series of shallow pools with little or no seepage in between.

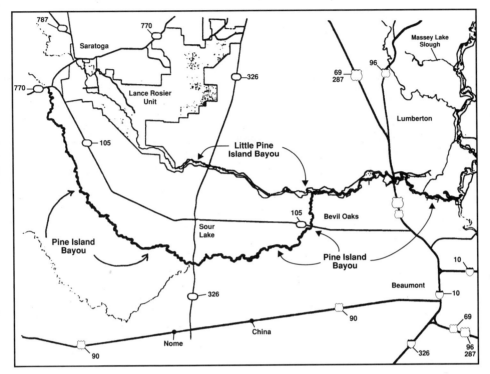

Pine Island Bayou

In wet periods the opposite is true. Then the entire stream, from well north of FM 770 all the way to the Neches, becomes a slowly moving swamp, a half-mile to nearly a mile wide. During a drought it can be hard to find the channel for cracked clay and mud; during a flood the channel is lost in a maze of hardwood forest and half-drowned palmetto palm. For some adventurous spirits that would be the best time to canoe the bayou. It would also be the easiest time to get lost there.

Assuming a wet season, there are five different trips down the bayou. The first (twenty-three miles) runs from FM 770 to State Highway 26 south of Sour Lake; the second (seven-and-one- half miles) meanders from State Highway 236 to a county road from Sour Lake to Beaumont (where the county road becomes Calder Lane); the third (seven miles) loops from the county road to State Highway 105; the fourth (thirteen miles) drifts from SH 105 to U.S. Highway 96/287/69 around the only development (Bevil Oaks) on the bayou; the last is an eight-mile float to the Neches River. On the last two trips Pine island Bayou forms Beaumont's north city limits. You would never know it. Very little development is visible from the bayou.

I recall coming across a story in a yellowed old newspaper about an engineer who resigned his position with a railroad construction company in the Thicket. "I'll be damned," he complained, "if I planned to build a railroad in the jungles of Africa." He must have been thinking of the Pine Island Bayou watershed. Even today it is remote and strange. The hardwood overstory shades endless thickets of palmetto palms, some shoulder high, some high as a rider's head on horseback. Tea-colored sloughs stretch back into dense growth, disappearing among the palmettos. Interspersed among mossed hardwoods are stands of cypress. It is hypnotic.

Sand and gravel bars form natural resting and camping places on the lower reaches of the bayou (particularly east of SH 326). Canoers should be aware both that in normal periods the stream channel is narrow, and that overhanging brush and limbs provide a challenge throughout virtually the entire trip. Towards the Neches River (essentially: east of SH 105) the water begins to have a brackish taint and the bayou begins to widen significantly. There is a boat ramp at the Highway 96 crossing. I hope it is obvious from the map that the final float (from 96 East) follows the southern border of the Beaumont Unit, all the way to the Neches.

Until its confluence with Little Pine Island Bayou (three miles east of the county road crossing), all of Pine Island Bayou is in private ownership. Night camping (as opposed to day use) anywhere in the Preserve requires a special National Park Service permit.

7

Future Green: A Rescue of Hope

Conservation in the Thicket has a past of respectable depth and a present which sums up a number of significant achievements. Now it is possible to visit the region—to hike, to camp, to canoe, even to ride horseback—without damaging a wilderness which otherwise surely would have been lost. But if all this has been achieved, why worry about the future? If the groundwork has been laid, why not sit back and let events take their course?

The reader already suspects the answer: in matters of ecology vs. economy, much backsliding is possible. The creation of units and parks and sanctuaries connected to stream corridors allows the lumber industry to continue harvesting trees and local people to continue in their ways, all the while maintaining real wilderness and its interconnections. This pattern, partly designed and partly stumbled onto, achieves a very important result: it allows man and nature, economics and ecology, to coexist. It goes without saying that any concept which can produce this result has an importance reaching far beyond itself.

As for the future, there is hope that in the broader Big Thicket region this complex of units-plus-corridors can be expanded. New units and corridors can be added; old corridors and units can be enlarged. Southeast Texas can thus become a network of valuable environmental areas connected and reinforced by hikeable, floatable, canoeable corridors, all without undercutting the economy of the region. Indeed, the economy will be improved by the addition of what Senator Ralph Yarborough envisioned long ago, namely, a tourism payroll to supplement income derived from timbering. All this could be done, this writer believes, without forcing a single family off its homesite or a single landowner to sell against his or her will.

In fact, this process—in different places and for different reasons—has already begun. What follows is both an account of this new beginning and a suggestion of where, in the long run, it might lead.

Parks and Refuges

Debates over conservation in the Thicket have largely left out the Trinity River. They have concentrated instead on the Neches River (into which Village Creek, Hickory Creek, Beech Creek, and Pine Island Bayou empty). With one exception the Thicket Preserve could have been called the Lower Neches River Basin Wilderness. This exception is the Menard Creek Corridor, which runs into the Trinity River not far from Romayor. Another exception might have been the Tanner Bayou Unit, suggested in the 1960s as part of a 35,000-acre Big Thicket "string of pearls." This area has not, however, been seriously proposed for inclusion in any park or refuge over the last three decades. Nor has any other.

What has been proposed along the Trinity River, and is in the process of being established, is the 1800-acre Davis Hill State Park and an adjacent national wildlife refuge of 20,000 acres immediately to its north. Taken together, these two areas—which will in important aspects be managed as one—have a combined area of 21,800 acres. This is not far in size from the Lance Rosier Unit of the Big Thicket Preserve, at 24,942 acres.

Davis Hill State Park was first proposed in the early 1980s by former U.S. Senator Price Daniel, but its land has only recently been purchased. Since funds for state park development are meager, it will be years before this area can be opened to the public. When opened, however, it will provide a rich combination of scenery, ecology, and recreation.

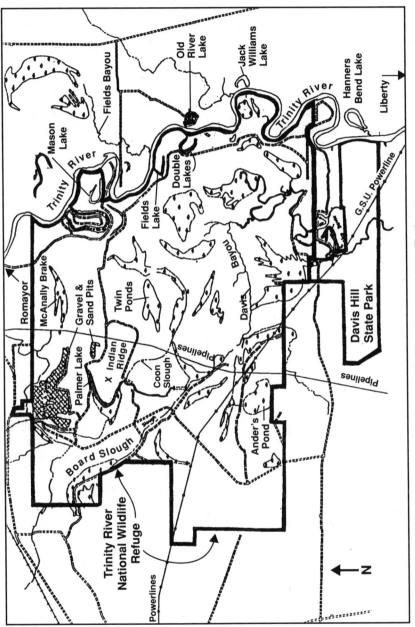

With few exceptions, Big Thicket country is flat. The western portion of the Davis Hill State Park, however, swells up abruptly from bottomlands roughly fifty-five feet above sea level, reaching a height of over 265 feet. Wooded and steeply rolling, Davis Hill is a salt dome, uplifted by subterranean pressures from a table-level plain. Like most salt domes, it sustains oil wells—but in this case only a few. On a clear day, I am told, a tree climb at the top of the hill allows one to see the Liberty County Court House, over fifteen miles to the south.

To the east of Davis Hill the parkland stretches through bottomland forest across cypress-lined Davis Bayou to the west bank of the Trinity River. The sandy banks there make an excellent place for swimming and fishing, as well as camping. The development plan for this park is, as noted above, a long way off. When completed it will almost certainly involve toilet, tenting and boat ramp facilities similar to those at Village Creek State Park. Also similar will be the efforts made to safeguard the habitat of rare, scarce, or unusual species.

Hunting (by permit) and hiking are allowed in a national wildlife refuge. Development, however, is not. This is good news for all who want to see significant areas of sheer wilderness retained and protected along the Trinity. The Trinity River National Wildlife Refuge—still seeking complete funding— will remain as wild as any unit of the Big Thicket Preserve. It is, moreover, less changed by lumbering than most preserve units. Some areas appear never to have been timbered at all.

The Davis Hill State Park, as described above, alternates between abrupt highlands and forest lowlands. The wildlife refuge consists of lowlands throughout, as the names of its physical features attest. First come the streams: Phillips Creek, Cherry Creek, Coon Slough, Board Slough, Davis Bayou, Nevel Bayou. These meander almost haphazardly, connecting lakes, swamps, and oxbows with names like Ander's Pond and Twin Ponds, McAnally Brake and Elbow Brake, Palmer Lake, Fields Lake, Double Lakes. In the northwest segment there is a low hammock called Indian Ridge, rising just south of abandoned sand and gravel pits. These, left to themselves, can become productive wildlife habitat. I know of one abandoned gravel pit

Cypress knees and tree overhang

near Romayor which has come to afford protection to both wading birds and alligators. The same can happen here.

Besides providing a sanctuary for game animals, the Trinity River Wildlife Refuge contains swamp thickets that make ideal rookeries for herons and egrets, and stands of ancient water oak and cypress that shelter songbirds and woodpeckers. One could easily imagine that bald eagles will return there, as they have along parts of the Neches River. The area is already a haven for hawks.

Donations and Consortia

Besides the adjacent state park and national wildlife refuge, other places have recently entered the list of protected areas in the Thicket. One fifty-acre area is located on the south side of the Pine Island Bayou Corridor not far west of the Highway 69 crossing. Another area, of eleven acres, is on the west bank of Village Creek just south of Highway 96. Formerly the Wilfred Turner Nature Sanctuary, it was donated to the National Park Service by the Magnolia Garden Club. It is, I am told, both a visually and a botanically rich area. Still another acreage—much larger than these two put together—is presently under discussion between the Park Service and its potential donor.

These areas are small, compared with Preserve units. But the fact that they are being donated now is of great importance. Almost certainly there will be more of such: padding a creek bank here, expanding a bayou greenbelt or a river corridor there, saving a swale or oxbow or swamp. The reason is economic. Almost without exception these donations will be in low places, on lands of no value for farming and little value for timbering due to their tendency toward heavy flooding. Very nearly the only economic use for such areas is as a sustainable basis for paying taxes. National wetlands legislation, moreover, makes it illegal to develop our nation's last remaining wetlands. One can expect, on these grounds alone, that many wetlands like those in the Thicket will be proposed for sanctuary status, whether through donation to private organizations or to agencies of federal, state, or even local governments.

Yes, local governments. I note that my own city of Denton, Texas, is entering into an agreement with the U.S. Corps of Engineers to purchase parts of a greenbelt corridor on the Elm Fork of the Trinity River, from Lake Ray Roberts, north of town, to Lake Dallas, towards Denton's east and south. This will make possible a nice canoeing stream as well as extensive hiking trails. The application of restoration ecology will allow the river corridor to revert back to something like its original botanical richness. My sense of the situation, however, is that the over-riding concern in this case has been the protection of the quality of Denton's future water supply. Most of Denton's water is now drawn from Lake Dallas, and a little common sense leads to the conclusion that badly placed, ill-planned development up-stream could easily foul these waters. In this case as in many others, ecological sense makes economic sense. A town that lacks clean water also lacks an economic future.

Besides federal wetlands legislation there is also federal flood insurance. That may seem to have little to do with either local government or wilderness, but in fact, it is aggravatingly relevant to both. Since the early days of the second Big Thicket movement, a number of "vacation subdivisions" and "wilder-ness estates" have been built in the Trinity River valley, ironi-cally drawn by the publicity generated to save the Big Thicket wilderness. Some of these are upscale suburban neighborhoods, others are patchworks of vacant lots next to lots containing small storage sheds, a cleared spot for a tent and a barbecue grill. Whether elaborate or plain, however, all of these real estate achievements flood. Since 1960 several "hundred year floods" (floods which ought, statistically, to occur only once per cen-tury) have overwhelmed the area, leaving open the joyous prospect of several more occurring in the near future.

One has to feel for the people who have invested their savings in these developments, only to see them inundated or washed away. Federal flood insurance, originally created to help people who live in areas which do not often flood, now is into the business of helping people who build in areas which flood ordinarily. The first time the Trinity River vacation estates flooded, this Federal fiscal help was greatly appreciated. After the second or third inundation, however, two new factors became clear to everyone. The cost of flood payments for rebuilding, already significant, were becoming astronomical, with the possibility of future rounds of still more inflated payments. It costs too much to perpetually rebuild/refurnish homes which will some day have to be rebuilt/refurnished again. The psychological cost of having to rebuild also began to take its toll. Even with federal subsidies for lowland home reconstruction, is it worth the effort? Will it be worth it the third, or fourth, or fifth time around?

One answer to this suggestion was proposed in 1992 by the county judge of Liberty County, Dempsie Henley—a gentleman already well known and well respected by Big Thicket conservationists. Henley suggested that the federal government (more specifically, FEMA, the Federal Emergency Management Agency) buy out all those floodplain subdivision landowners *who would like to be bought out*. His objective was not to stage one more raid on a beleaguered federal treasury, but to save the federal government money in the longer run. That Henley's plea was met by sign-carrying protesters complaining that the feds were about to take over their homes shows how little he was understood. His concern was with willing sellers, and no one else.

As this is being written, the outcome of Henley's effort remains—like much in the Big Thicket area—uncertain. His plea, however, points up a fundamental fact. The cost of federal flood insurance provides yet another good reason to create wild or semi-wild greenbelts along area streams. It also provides a cogent argument for heading off development in lowlands which will inevitably flood. It also suggests the possibility that, whether through scenic easements, donations, or purchases from willing sellers, a greenbelt could be built up along the lower Trinity River to preserve it for the future, as both a recreational and a wilderness resource. Economic pressures suggest such an outcome. Interestingly, they do not suggest that any such outcome be achieved by government condemnation or forced purchase of land.

There is one more factor to consider. In July, 1978, the Dujay Sanctuary was formally dedicated. Consisting of forty wooded acres contiguous to the northeastern section of the Lance Rosier Unit on the Black Creek Road, this sanctuary belongs to Lamar University and is scheduled for educational and scientific uses. No full-scale search of land records in the region has been attempted, but it is known that Rice University owns eighty acres fronting on Highway 770 adjacent to the Rosier Unit, while Baylor University owns a tract on Pine Island Bayou adjacent to the Highway 770 crossing. These and other possible university-owned lands in the area could be managed as a "consortium": a sort of gentleman's agreement to maintain the basic ecology of each area while making possible joint scientific and educational uses. Not only would such an arrangement benefit each of these universities, but it also suggests another potential set of institutions to which land might eventually be donated in the Thicket region. Besides Rice, Baylor, and Lamar there are, in the immediate vicinity, the University of Houston, Sam Houston State University, and Stephen F. Austin State University.

The Big Thicket Addition Bill

In the last chapter a great deal was said about Congressman Charles Wilson's "Big Thicket Addition Bill," which would have added the Big Sandy-Village Creek Corridor and the Upper Neches Canyonlands to the preserve. As this is written, the addition bill has not passed. Or rather, it has passed both houses of Congress, *and still not passed.*

A few words of explanation are in order.

On November 23, 1991, the U.S. House of Representatives passed HR1592, Wilson's addition bill, and on February 19, 1992, a second set of Senate hearings was held.

These hearings were a *pro forma* affair, with both sides agreeing to let previous Senate hearing testimony reflect their views. Those involved with the bill thought that the matter was on the verge of immediate resolution. But affairs dragged on.

Weeks passed before Senators Gramm and Bentsen finally met and resolved their differences to produce a unified bill.

Then began the Big Wait. By mid-May, 1992, conservationists began to realize that time was not on their side. They saw that recesses for holidays and for fall election campaigns would leave little time for Senate action. On June 1, twenty-five to thirty environmental groups and around forty individuals were prevailed upon to send telegrams to the senators, urging haste. From then through September, telephone calls were made weekly to the senators' aides asking about the addition bill's status.

The problem, environmentalists were told, lay in the Senate Energy and Natural Resources Committee, which was tied up with "controversial" legislation. The committee staff, in its deep wisdom, wanted to wait and bring up the Thicket bill later, with other "noncontroversial" bills. Sure enough, they did. That is, they waited.

In August word came down that a language barrier stood in the way of passage. It had been an early agreement that land taken from lumber companies along the Big Sandy-Village Creek Corridor would be compensated for by land taken from National Forests farther north in East Texas. The trade was not to be made acre for acre, but instead according to the value of land taken at its "highest and best use," and therein lay the supposed language problem. Conservationists, along with the Big Thicket National Preserve's land acquisition officer, pointed out vigorously (one might almost say "exasperatedly") that such language had already been included in other legislation without creating semantic misery, that "highest and best use" was already standard operating procedure and hence a non-issue. Senator Gramm and lumber company officials were eventually placated by being asked to add statements to the Senate report on the Big Thicket.

It was hard to imagine that anything was left which could delay passage. In this case, it seemed that conservationists lacked imagination. After Labor Day Senators John Glenn (D-Ohio), Howard Metzenbaum (D-Ohio), and Jake Garn (R-Utah) held hostage all bills in the committee, pending passage of pet bills of their own. Other senators on the committee proved their capacity for useless vacuity by filibustering.

Finally, on October 8, the Big Thicket Addition Bill sneaked out of the Senate Energy and Natural Resources Committee and was passed by the Senate. By now, at the very end of the session, with Congressmen and Senators poised to rush to their districts to campaign, it was too late to get a House-Senate conference committee to iron out differences between the House and Senate bills. Congressman Wilson had made arrangements for the House to pass the Senate bill on the consent calendar, an arrangement which allows a skeleton crew of remaining congressmen to make speeches and pass entirely noncontroversial legislation through a unanimous vote.

It had always been specified that a single congressman could halt the consent calendar by voting "no" on any proposed legislation, but in the entire history of Congress this veto had never been used. Sure enough, William Dannemeyer, (R-Cal.), a one term congressman, remained in Washington after recess and personally vetoed 70 bills (including the Thicket addition) by not agreeing to unanimous consent. Not only did he kill 70 bills, but he also refused to let representatives who were leaving Congress for the last time give brief farewell speeches for the record. No one could believe it.

The congressman, a one-termer who had never passed a piece of legislation in office and had failed in a bid to run for the United States Senate from California, told reporters that he hated Washington and everyone and everything in it. His only goal had been to destroy as much as he could before he left.

The book is not closed on the Big Thicket addition, however, in spite of efforts to shut it. Massive infusions of aid by the Republican Party failed to elect Congressman Wilson's opponent in the November, 1992, elections. Wilson returned to office with increased seniority, determined to pass his bill in the next session of Congress. On the surface, at least, no obstacles to its passage seems to exist. Wilson's addition bill has already passed both houses; the new administration seems more favorably inclined towards environmental legislation; the relevant House and Senate Committees are already primed to act. Given Congress' previous track record, however, one hesitates to make

Cypress Swamp

any shining predictions. Time, and the welter of politics, will tell.

Besides the obvious ecological reasons for passing the Thicket addition bill, there are economic factors. Congressman Wilson's bill not only ties together wilderness areas that otherwise would be left dangling, it also incorporates the Blue Elbow Swamp at Orange, Texas, on Interstate Highway 10. It is this area, included in the House but not in the Senate "addition" bill, which required—but did not receive—a House/Senate conference committee at the tail end of the 1992 congressional session. Blue Elbow was a late addition to the congressman's bill, along with a smaller area on the Neches river across from its confluence with Village Creek. They were not in the bill as first passed by the U.S. House of Representatives, but were in the second version. Hopefully, they will be included also in the third—if and when it passes.

I have noted that the proposed Blue Elbow Unit is on Interstate 10. This does not affect its environmental value. In the Big Thicket National Preserve there are less than 200 acres of cypress, tupelo, and cypress-tupelo swamps, all-told. Blue Elbow's 3592 acres, though they are only now beginning to recover from the savage timbering methods of the 1930s and 40s, are almost entirely cypress and/or tupelo swamp, thus adding to the Preserve's inventory of plant associations. They are also a refuge for alligators, river otters, hawks, muskrat, nutria, and every conceivable kind of wading bird. The last time I was there I saw a bald eagle, perched on a dead cypress limb, spreading its massive wings to the morning sun.

Interstate 10 only traverses the far southern tip of Blue Elbow. But that traverse is important. Several million cars per year pour down I-10, from New Orleans to Houston and points west, from Houston and its environs east to New Orleans, Gulfport, and North Florida. If even one-fourth of these visitors could be beguiled into stopping at Blue Elbow for a canoe or houseboat ride, or for an hour at a National Park Service Big Thicket Visitors' Center, some would remain to eat at local restaurants, explore Orange's museums, and even sleep at local motels. Still others would consider motoring up into southeast Texas to see the Big Thicket National Preserve or take advantage of adjacent state parks. (The creation of a new twenty-nine-acre Big Thicket Preserve Museum and Visitors Center on Highway 69 at FM 420, seven miles north of Kountz—already starting to take form—will make tourism in the area all the easier.)

The end result could be a very real boost for a regional economy that could use it. The goal of environmentalism, of course, is the protection of the living web which sustains us on this planet. It is not to "make money." But if a farsighted environmental policy can also help sustain a local economy, that is all the better.

One final note. The last time the writer asked, an ordinary alligator was worth $18 per foot on the black market. That price creates a powerful temptation for poachers, one which is generally not resisted around Orange and the Sabine River. Specifically, it is not resisted in Blue Elbow Swamp. Texas game wardens have the task of enforcing laws against poaching, but, like everyone else, wardens have a severe interest in protecting their own health. The swamps and sloughs and the river around Orange are dangerous at night. There seems to be a competition between drug runners and poachers to keep it that way. When and if Blue Elbow becomes part of the Big Thicket National Preserve, the first order of business (after land acquisition, which should be straightforward, seeing that Blue Elbow has a willing seller) will be to enforce the game laws. As things now stand, the largest alligators there reach only four, perhaps five feet in length. Environmentalists, airboat proprietors, and visitors from Europe and the Pacific Rim deserve to see *Alligator Mississipiensis* at a size closer to its native bulk. A fullgrown alligator can easily reach ten to fifteen feet in length.

Changing Policies: Clearcutting Lost, Corridors Regained?

All the instruments used to safeguard wilderness in the Big Thicket are important. Sanctuaries, parks, refuges, units, corridors, and consortia make a blessed patchwork which can assure the preservation of otherwise extinguished species, the continued existence of free-flowing streams, the perpetuation of the sounds and sights and smells of wilderness.

But they are scarcely the whole story. By far the greater part of forested land in Southeast Texas belongs neither to small landowners nor to governments and environmental groups, but to large lumber companies. It is these which, beginning in the 1940s and then accelerating from the 1950s to the present, have pursued clearcutting policies which have transformed hundreds of thousands of lush, diverse Big Thicket acres into pine monoculture: rows of pine and nothing else, in many cases from horizon to horizon. More often than not such policies include draining of wetlands, bulldozing of creeks, dumping of refuse into streams. Most Texans, to be sure, are unaware of this transformation, and of its incredible sweep. But for groups seemingly as different as hunters, chambers of commerce, and environmentalists, this ceaseless denuding of the state's forest belt appears as an increasing disaster. In the end, and for the great bulk of the Lone Star State's twelve-and-a-half million

Clearcut with burnt timber: aerial view

acres of prime forest land, what will be left? Certainly not squirrels, raccoons, and possums. Of course not ferns, and orchids, and wild birds. Beyond a doubt little that anyone would want to drive fifty, or a hundred, or two hundred miles to see.

Against this backdrop of massive, destructive change, the achievements of conservationists seem small indeed: mere green fly specks against an immense and growing industrial emptiness. The great long-term problem lies in lumber company policies. The real long-term solution must lie in having those policies changed.

It appears to this writer, after much reading and much conversing with representatives of the forest products industry, that change is in the air. Perhaps what follows will exaggerate the degree of this transformation. But it does appear as if at least the major lumber companies in Southeast Texas are beginning to change their clearcutting policies for the better.

The three largest forest landowners in the Big Thicket area are Temple-Inland, Champion International, and Louisiana Pacific. The largest, Temple-Inland, has virtually absorbed the former Eastex Corporation and owns over a million acres of Texas forest. Louisiana Pacific has absorbed Kirby Enterprises. Champion International has long been the possessor of large blocks of Texas real estate. It has absorbed both Southland Corporation and St. Regis.

Each of these massive corporate interests is presently announcing new clearcutting policies; in each case the stated goal is, if not to give up clearcutting entirely, then to limit its extent. Finally, each is setting aside unique areas in their forests, protecting them from clearcutting and often from cutting of any kind. No such policies were imagined, pursued or proposed when the second Big Thicket drive began in the early 1960s. But they now seem to be coming into existence.

This shift is probably clearest in the case of Temple-Inland, whose new Best Use Policy reflects both changing economic factors and an increased level of response to public pressure. The most important part of this response is a new attitude towards hardwoods and the bottomlands in which they grow. There is now a steady demand for furniture grade hardwood, a demand which was not as significant in past decades. Such hardwood can not be grown in twenty to twenty-five-year cycles, as can pulp pine. The result is that Temple-Inland will be letting bottomland hardwood forests grow forty to fifty years before harvesting them. In the rainy confines of Southeast Texas, a forty or fifty-year-old forest is well-developed indeed. It is no small thing that, as Temple-Inland envisions the future, hunters, birdwatchers, fishermen and research biologists will be able to look forward to the existence of mature hardwood forests along area streams. So will their children and grandchildren. This prospect goes beyond preservation of existing hardwood stream corridors. To satisfy the projected demand for furniture grade hardwoods, many areas which have been transformed into mixed pine-hardwood stands will be allowed to return to pure hardwood, more suited to the native terrain.

There is a catch in this, of course. Up through the 1970s Temple-Inland (then Temple Industries) was the only large lumber company that did not clearcut. In recent years the home-based corporation began to accept clearcutting as a method, and has plans to cut the old-growth hardwoods on its lands. Many of us think this is very bad news, indeed. On the positive side, Temple-Inland has set aside "environmental management zones" along streams in uniquely rich botanical areas: Wild Azalea Canyon, Scrappin Valley, North and South Boggy Sloughs. In these zones only selective cutting is allowed. In most of them "skidders" are not used; downed trees have to be lifted out, carefully. All this is well and good. But what will happen to the old-growth, ancient hardwoods on Temple-Inland acreage? The answer will not satisfy many, but it is a better one than this writer would have expected in the present context. The new hardwood clearcuts will average thirty acres, thus forestalling massive horizon-to-horizon devastation of entire bottomlands. They will be narrow and winding, a boon to game and other wildlife species, which benefit from the presence of forest "edges." And they will be replaced by future hardwood forests of the type growing there originally. Presumably the result will be a more vertical, less gnarled, economically more valuable forest.

Faced with the distracting combination of new, more enlightened forest management policies hooked incongruously to the cutting of remaining ancient hardwood stands, one likely conservationist response will be to urge Temple-Inland to create more of both the "environmental management zones" and the adjacent "sanctuaries" of big, old-growth hardwoods.

In urging such action they could point to Champion International's recent "Special Places in the Woods" program, a process of setting aside unique woodland areas which is already well under way and shows every sign of continuing. So far Champion has set aside ten of these, the majority of which are in the original Big Thicket area. Most impressive to this writer is the 300-acre hardwood corridor along Batiste Creek north of Devers in Liberty County. This swampy area contains an interesting overlap of species common to both the Lower Thicket and the Gulf Coastal prairie, thus in effect adding to the catalog of protected plants and animals represented by the Big Thicket National Preserve. Other "special places" include 320 acres along Kickapoo Creek in Trinity and Polk Counties (an area noted for both its wildlife and its unusual rock outcrops); Dillard Creek, a 270-acre corridor west of Trinity in Walker county; the seventy-nine-acre Beech-Magnolia Canyons on Vincent Creek in Tyler County; the Beaver Pond, a forty-acre area on Nettles Cemetery Road; the nearly 100-acre Blue Heron Rookery just off White Rock Creek near Groveton, in Trinity County; the 145-acre Apolonia Trail, eight miles east of Anderson in Grimes County, which mingles East Texas and Central Texas vegetation much as the Batiste Creek corridor mingles Thicket and prairie species; the Carter Sand and Water Stop, a fourteen-acre longleaf pine and springfed bog locale on a now abandoned railroad spur; the Oyster Reefs, a 315-acre outcrop of fossil oyster reefs in White Rock Creek in Trinity County; the wooded fifty-acre Mission Señora de la Purisima Concepcion site near the Angelina River in Nacogdoches County. Besides these sites, Champion International is in the process of setting up two others, an Indian massacre site north of Crockett, in Houston County, and a wooded area on the Neches River east of Corrigan.

Two points might be noted about these "special places." Almost without exception they are wetlands, or "sanctuaries" alongside wetlands, thus bearing out the thesis that such areas are increasingly going to tend towards protected natural areas. The second point is that Champion's special places are not public parks or playgrounds, although Champion will doubtless be willing to allow certain groups special access. These nature sanctuaries remain privately owned, however, and should not be entered without permission.

Exceptions to this rule include three woodland trails which Champion makes open to the public: the Longleaf Pine Trail, a two-mile loop including a large stand of virgin longleaf pines (three miles east of Camden on Farm Road 62); the two-mile Moscow Trail, which follows the meanders of Long King Creek (just off U.S. Highway 59 one mile south of Moscow); and the 1.5-mile Bull Creek Trail (8.5 miles west of Corrigan off of U.S. Highway 287). These are not hard to find. Both trailheads and trails are well marked.

One would have to be blind not to see the virtue of these newly created "special places," and more than a little sour-tempered not to applaud their creation. Whether they represent a real change in attitude, rather than a mere public relations ploy (but a pretty good ploy, at over 1600 acres!) depends upon Champion International's policies towards clearcutting and towards bottomland hardwoods. According to those the author has talked to at Champion, the size of clearcuts is being reduced and the width of streamside zones increased. For fifteen years Champion has been leaving hardwood "stringers" along even intermittent streams. For the last three years these have been expanded.

The situation with Louisiana-Pacific appears still more straightforward. Two years ago as of this writing, L.-P. publicly renounced clearcutting in California. On its over 650,000 Texas acres this corporation has not used clearcutting as a basic tool. Instead it has practiced "selective harvesting": tree-by-tree rather than whole-forest removal.

Even if this portrayal of the policies of the Texas forest products interests may seem enthusiastic and optimistic, the facts sketched above do show that there has been a real change of perspective and behavior by major lumber companies. Things have changed, not as fully as this writer would wish, but the change is real.

It is interesting to speculate on the causes of this new attitude, not only for curiosity's sake, but to test whether the change is superficial, and whether it will last. There is, to begin with, a new generation of foresters in the field, a generation not always happy with the "scorched earth" policies of their predecessors and more willing to save a creekbank or a swamp or a clump of old hardwoods. Many did not like the regulations under which they were formerly compelled to work, and are pleased with changes. There is also a profounder awareness of environmental problems (and values) among many, but not all, corporate executives. A quietly rising tide of ecological awareness has seeped into the managerial offices and corporate board rooms of the lumber industry. But the corporate mergers, countermergers, and other economic wars of the 1980s have thrust some managers into power who are decidedly non-green. The result is a mixed bag, though, at least it is my impression, green is now a more acceptable color among forest product executives than it was a generation, or even a decade, ago.

Three more causes probably should be added. Public pressure is among them, and not only from the Sierra Club and Earth First. Tourism in the piney woods is not exactly encouraged by acre after acre of bare loam and windrows of burning limbs, stumps, and branches. Motel owners, restaurateurs, mom and pop service station operators are scarcely enriched by mile after mile of cutover land—some of it left unplanted year after year— if this slows the flow of visitors to East Texas. There are also those local people who simply love the piney woods, and don't want to see them scalped. Among these are many hunters, whose voices tend to be heard when those of specifically environmental organizations are not. Lumber companies may deny that they listen to the voice of the public, but in fact they are not deaf.

More immediate and more "realistic" causes for lumber companies' changes in attitude include the demand for furniture-quality hardwood—already mentioned above—as well as the fear that if they do not mend their own ways, federal legislation will do it for them. The public uproar over the cutting of old-growth timber and the possible extinction of the Pacific Northwest's spotted owl has had its effect on forest product industries everywhere. East Texas is no exception. Possibly more important in this regard has been the Environmental Protection Agency which, over the last decade, has moved quietly behind the scenes, warning lumber companies that unless their practices were brought within acceptable limits, the E.P.A. might be forced to step in. The suits of the Texas Committee on Natural Resources and its allies to halt clearcutting in Texas national forests have also had an effect. (From national forest land to lumber company land is often only a matter of a few feet.)

So there is a change: the beginnings, at any rate, of policies which will be kinder to the land, less destructive of soils, streams, and hardwoods. How far these policies will go towards sustaining forest habitats and the creatures that live in them remains to be seen. Hunters, environmentalists, proprietors and tourists need to understand that a change is taking place. They also need to remain skeptical. Understanding is essential; but so is the will to keep up persistent pressure. If eternal vigilance is the price of liberty, it is the price of ecology also.

Some might say that the new policies and attitudes come too late. It is easy *now* for timber interests to begin talking about protecting streambanks and "saving the ecology." They have already done so much damage, some will protest, that future policies are a moot point.

I would be a lot happier if I could believe there is not a lot of truth in this objection. The dreariest afternoon I ever spent elapsed last summer as I drove east from the southern tip of the Turkey Creek Unit through mile after mile after mile of clearcut country towards Highway 92. The clearcuts there extended to the northern and eastern horizons: barren, ugly, and monotonous. There were occasional "stringers" of hardwoods along infrequent meandering creekbeds. They were one tree wide, and many of the trees were damaged. Perhaps lumber companies will be widening such stringers. Apparently the message had not gotten through to the field crews here. Occasional sentinel hardwoods had been left out in the barrenness, for reasons none too clear. Some would live, while others, damaged and isolated, would die. The first thought was: Why bother? What was the point? Would these "stringers" ever be more than one tree wide? Would squirrels, or raccoons, or woodpeckers ever live in these lonely, isolated trees? Would people in their right minds ever want to drive, or hike, or birdwatch here?

I never got to Highway 92. I turned back and, instead, drove north along the margins of the Turkey Creek Unit. There I found a new set of problems to worry over. The National Park Service is beginning to work on a Partnership for Preservation program, designed to spread the notion that stewardship in areas adjacent to national parks, and to areas like the Big Thicket National Preserve, is in the landowner's interest. After all, the argument runs, to allow some hardwoods to remain beyond preserve boundaries, to protect a creek, to safeguard a fern valley or a baygall, will enhance the value of the owner's land. Formal agreements (scenic easements for example) are possible. But so are verbal agreements. So is a simple determination to keep one's land beautiful, and green, and diverse.

To accomplish this, park service employees will be contacting local mayors, county judges, commissioners, and chambers of commerce. Public meetings will be held throughout the regions to discuss the value of stewardship and to air problems (real or imagined) with the Park Service. It is hard to imagine a better idea. Preserve units and corridors do not do well as biological islands in a sea of pine monoculture; they fare better when their borders are more diffuse-that is, when some hardwoods are left growing near their perimeters, when "stringers" are left on creeks that flow into or out of their expanse. Partnership for Preservation ought to be pursued not just once or temporarily, but persistently. The end results would be worth it.

But why limit one's talk to mayors, county judges, and chambers of commerce? The dialogue needs to take place first with lumber interests. In many places of the Turkey Creek Unit, lumber companies have scalped the earth right up to the Preserve's boundaries. Exactly the same thing has happened to the Jack Gore Baygall Unit and to the Neches River Corridor. Lumber companies, new policies notwithstanding, assert their ownership by isolating the preserves to the fullest extent. Surely some less destructive process is possible. This writer is not talking about forbidding anyone to harvest trees. But couldn't a straggle of hardwoods be left at preserve boundaries? Or would this—as we have so often been told in similar circumstances— undermine the economy of East Texas, wreck Life as We Have Known It, and destroy the Boy Scout Creed? Funny thing: for some reason this writer tends to doubt it.

When I first began writing about the Big Thicket, in the early 1960s, tens of thousands of acres that are now pulp pine deserts were rich, varied Big Thicket forests. The loss since then has been immense, and in many ways is irreversible. But there is another way of looking at the situation, both more hopeful and more instructive. When the second Big Thicket movement began in the early 1960s there was no public revulsion against clearcutting; nor was there a shred of restraint in the applica- tion of this new timber technology. Every swamp was to be drained if it could be; trees were cut on creekbanks and unsalable trunks, branches, and brush were bulldozed into the creeks; clearcuts sprawled over four, six, eight thousand acres; rare, scarce, endangered species were eliminated along with the most common, and at the rate at which the pillage was proceed- ing it was only a question of time, not only until the Big Thicket lost its biological identity, but also until southeast Texas be- came a biological desert, from Interstate 45 to the Sabine River. Just how much time it would take was not clear. But the process was on its way, and nothing whatsoever showed the slightest sign of stopping it.

But if one takes the long view, a corner has been turned. The great, overriding hope is that through the preservation of hardwood stream corridors, otherwise disjunct, isolated areas can be joined into a cohesive, self-sustaining pattern. There is a chance now for wetlands, for corridors, parks, sanctuaries, preserves; and for reptiles, songbirds, orchids, seeps, bayous,

An Insectivore: Bladderwort

baygalls, eagles; and for river otters, alligators, deer, butterflies, mushrooms and a thousand other kinds of flying, crawling, growing, and singing things.

Though this goal has been only partly achieved, the moral is clear—it is infinitely better than what could have happened. Infinitely more hopeful, overwhelmingly more living. For those who have struggled, and will continue to struggle, to make it so, there is not only joy but a profound consolation. In a world where good causes often die and honest hopes lose themselves in sheer futility, something lasting and living has been actually achieved.

People tried, and it mattered.

Appendix

Representative Flora and Fauna of the Big Thicket

Trees and Shrubs

1. Upland communities

Trees

Longleaf Pine	*Pinus palustris*
Shortleaf Pine	*Pinus echinata*
Sweetgum	*Liquidambar Styraciflua*
Blackjack Oak	*Quercus marilandica*
Bluejack Oak	*Quercus incana*
Post Oak	*Quercus stellata*
Black Hickory	*Carya texana*
Shagbark Hickory	*Carya ovata*
Winged Elm	*Ulmus alata*
Black Cherry	*Prunus serotina*
Sugarberry	*Celtis laevigate*

Shrubs and small trees

American Plum	*Prunus americana*
Flatwoods Plum	*Prunus umbellata*
Carolina Holly	*Ilex ambigua*
Georgia Holly	*Ilex longipes*
Parsley Hawthorn	*Crataegus Marshallii*

[193]

Allegheny Chinquapin	*Castanea pumila*
Eastern Redbud	*Cercis canadensis*
Tree Sparkleberry	*Vaccinium arboreum*
Pawpaw	*Asimina triloba*
Rusty Blackhaw	*Viburnum rufidulum*

2. Beech-magnolia communities

Trees

Beech	*Fagus grandifolia*
Southern Magnolia	*Magnolia grandiflora*
Loblolly Pine	*Pinus taeda*
Swamp Chestnut Oak	*Quercus Michauxii*
White Oak	*Quercus alba*
Sugar Maple	*Acer saccharum*
Mockernut Hickory	*Carya tomentosa*
Shagbark Hickory	*Carya ovata*
White Ash	*Fraxinus americana*
Carolina Basswood	*Tilia caroliniana*
American Holly	*Ilex opaca*
Shumard Oak	*Quercus Shumardii*

(The beech-magnolia community is taken by Professor Claude McLeod to define the Upper Thicket; in the Lower Thicket beech is largely replaced by swamp chestnut oak to create a swamp chestnut oak-magnolia community. These two nearly identical communities constitute a "matrix vegetation" linking all other Big Thicket plant communities together.)

Shrubs and small trees

Redbay	*Persea borbonia*
Common Sweatleaf	*Symplocos tinctoria*
Witchhazel	*Hamamelis virginiana*
American Snowbell	*Styrax americana*
Yaupon	*Ilex vomitoria*

Two-wing Silverbell	*Halesia diptera*
Kentucky Wisteria	*Wisteria frutescens*
Arrowwood Viburnum	*Viburnum dentatum*
Mapleleaf Viburnum	*Viburnum acerifolium*
Carolina Buckthorn	*Rhamnus caroliniana*
Inkberry	*Ilex glabra*
Swamp Cyrilla	*Cyrilla racemiflora*

(Most of these shrubs and small trees create an "understory" throughout the areas of Big Thicket matrix vegetation. Arrowwood viburnum and Carolina buckthorn are more frequent in the Upper Thicket, mapleleaf viburnum, inkberry, and swamp cyrilla in the Lower Thicket.)

3. Savannah communities

Trees

Longleaf Pine	*Pinus palustris*

Shrubs and small trees

Southern Waxmyrtle	*Myrica cerifera*

4. Bog communities

Trees

Sweetbay Magnolia	*Magnolia virginiana*
Swamp Tupelo	*Nyssa sylvatica var. biflora*

Shrubs and small trees

Piedmont Azalea	*Rhododendron canascens*
Inkberry	*Ilex glabra*
He-huckleberry	*Lyonia ligustrina*

Rabbiteye Blueberry   *Vaccinium virgatum*
Poison-Sumac   *Rhus vernix*

5. Palmetto-baldcypress-hardwood communities

Trees

Baldcypress   *Taxodium distichum*
Water Oak   *Quercus nigra*
Willow Oak   *Quercus phellos*

Shrubs and small trees

Dwarf Palmetto   *Sabal minor*

6. Baygall communities

Trees

Sweetbay Magnolia   *Magnolia virginiana*
Redbay   *Persea Borbonia*
Water Oak   *Quercus nigra*
Blackgum   *Nyssa sylvatica*
Carolina Ash   *Fraxinus caroliniana*

Shrubs and small trees

Common Buttonbush   *Cephalanthus occidentalis*
Possumhaw Viburnum   *Viburnum nudum*
Gallberry   *Ilex coriacea*

7. Floodplain forest communities

Trees

Baldcypress	*Taxodium distichum*
Water Tupelo	*Nyssa aquatica*

8. Streambank communities

Trees

River Birch	*Betula nigra*
American Sycamore	*Platanus occidentalis*
Boxelder	*Acer negundo*
Planertree	*Planera aquatica*
American Elm	*Ulmus Americana*
Cherrybark Oak	*Quercus falcata var. pagodaefolia*
Overcup Oak	*Quercus lyrata*

Shrubs and small trees

Black Willow	*Salix nigra*
Blueberry Hawthorn	*Crataegus brachyacantha*
American Elder	*Sambucus canadensis*
Hazel Alder	*Alnus serrulata*
Possumhaw Holly	*Ilex decidua*
Strawberry Bush	*Euonymous americanus*
Fringe-tree	*Chionanthus virginica*
Honeylocust	*Gleditsia triacanthos*
He-huckleberry	*Lyonia ligustrina*
Virginia Sweetspire	*Itea virginica*
American Snowbell	*Styrax americana*
Sebastian's Spurge	*Sebastiania fruticosa*

Ferns

Cutleaf Grape Fern	*Botrychium dissectum (occasional)*
Virginia Grape Fern	*Botrychium virginianum (rather frequent)*
Bulbous Adder's-Tongue	*Ophioglossum crotalophoroides (rare)*
Limestone Adder's-Tongue	*Ophioglossum Engelmannii (uncommon)*
Fragile Adder's-Tongue	*Ophioglossum nudicaule (rare)*
*Adder's Tongue	*Ophioglossum vulgatum (uncommon)*
Cinnamon Fern	*Osmunda cinnamonea (frequent where found)*
Royal Fern	*Osmunda regalis var. spectabilis (frequent where found)*
xJapanese Climbing Fern	*Lygodium japonicum (occasional)*
xSword Fern	*Nephrolepis exaltata (rare if escaped)*
Bracken	*Pteridium aquilinum var. pseudocaudatum (only infrequent)*
xSpider Brake	*Pteris multifida (rare)*
Alabama Lipfern	*Cheilanthes alabamensis (infrequent)*
Wooly Lipfern	*Cheilanthes tomentosa (rare)*
Sensitive Chainfern	*Onoclea sensibilis (frequent)*
Virginia Chainfern	*Woodwardia virginica (rather frequent)*
Chain Fern	*Lorinsera areolata*

Ebony Spleenwort	*Asplenium platyneuron (rather common)*
Little Ebony Spleenwort	*Asplenium resiliens (rare if present)*
Southern Lady-Fern	*Athyrium Felis-femina var. asplenioides (rather frequent)*
Blunt-Lobed Woodsia	*Woodsia obtusa (occasional)*
Downy Shieldfern	*Thelypteris dentata (occasional)*
Broad Beech Fern	*Thelypteris hexagonoptera (rare)*
Southern Shieldfern	*Thelypteris Kunthii (occasional)*
x	*Thelypteris Torresiana (rare)*
Marsh Shieldfern	*Thelypteris palustris var. Haleana (rare)*
x	*Thelypteris versicolor (rare)*
Florida Shieldfern	*Dryopteris ludoviciana (recently discovered)*
Christmas Fern	*Polystichum acrostichoides (infrequent)*
Resurrection Fern	*Polypodium polypodioides var. Michauxianum (common on trees)*
Water Fern	*Azotla caroliniana (common where found)*

This list is compiled from Cory and Parks *Biological Survey of the East Texas Big Thicket Area, 1938*; from Donovan S. Correll, *Ferns and Fern Allies of Texas*, Renner, Texas: Texas Research Foundation, 1956; and from John K. Small, *Ferns of the Southeastern States*, Lancaster, Pa.: The Science Press, 1938. The help of Professor Correll and Geraldine Watson in compiling this list is deeply appreciated. An "x" to the left of a name indicates that the species in question is not indigenous to Texas, though it may be naturalized there. An asterisk indicates the *possibility* of the existence of a species in the Big Thicket.

Fern Allies

Whisk Fern	*Psilotum nudum*
Tall Souring-Rush	*Equisetum hyemale var. affine (occasional)*
Southern Club-Moss	*Lycopodium adpressum (occasional)*
Foxtail Club-Moss	*Lycopodium alopercuroides (occasional)*
Carolina Club-Moss	*Lycopodium carolinianum (very rare)*
Meadow Spike-Moss	*Selaginella apoda (occasional)*
Riddell's Selaginella	*Selaginella Riddellii (common where found)*
Quillwort	*Isoetes melanopoda (rare)*

Orchids

Yellow Lady's-Slipper	*Cypripedium Calceolus var. pubescens (rare)*
White Fringed Orchid	*Habenaria Blephariglottis (uncommon)*
Chapman's Orchid	*Habernaria Chapmanii (rare)*
Yellow Fringed Orchid	*Habenaria ciliaris (uncommon)*
Green Rein-Orchid	*Habenaria clavellata (frequent)*
Crested Fringed Orchid	*Habenaria cristata (rare)*
Southern Rein-Orchid	*Habenaria flava (rare)*
Yellow Fringeless Orchid	*Habenaria integra (rare)*
Ragged Fringed Orchid	*Habenaria lacera*
Snowy Orchid	*Habenaria nivea (infrequent)*

Long-horned Habenaria	*Habenaria quinqueseta (probably extinct)*
Water Spider Orchid	*Habenaria repens (frequent where found)*
Snakemouth	*Pogonia ophioglossiodes (uncommon)*
*Spreading Pogonia	*Cleistes divaricata (doubtful in Texas)*
*Three Birds	*Triphora trianthophora (rare)*
Large Whorled Pogonia	*Isotria verticillata (occasional)*
Little Ladies' Tresses	*Spiranthes Grayi*
Fragrant Ladies' Tresses	*Spiranthes cernua var. odorata (rare)*
Nodding Ladies' Tresses	*Spiranthes cernua var. cernua*
Slender Ladies' Tresses	*Spiranthes gracilis (rather frequent)*
Florida Ladies' Tresses	*Spiranthes gracilis var. floridiana (rare)*
Lace-Lip Spiral-Orchid	*Spiranthes X laciniata (rare)*
Giant Spiral Orchid	*Spiranthes longilabris (rare)*
Oval Ladies' Tresses	*Spiranthes ovalis (rare)*
Giant Ladies' Tresses	*Spiranthes praecox (occasional)*
Spring Ladies' Tresses	*Spiranthes vernalis (rather frequent)*
*Low Erythrodes	*Erythrodes querceticola (very rare if in Texas)*
Southern Twayblade	*Listeria australis (frequent where found)*
Bearded Grass-Pink	*Calopogon barbatus (very rare)*
Grass-Pink Orchid	*Calopogon pulchellus (uncommon)*
Spring Coral Root	*Corallorhiza wisteriana (occasional)*

Crane-Fly Orchid	*Tipularia discolor (uncommon)*	
Green Addersmouth	*Malaxis unifolia (uncommon)*	
Crested Coral Root	*Hexalectris spicata (rare, recently discovered)*	
Shadowwitch	*Ponthieva racemosa (very rare)*	

This list is compiled from Cory and Parks *Biological Survey of the East Texas Big Thicket Area (1938);* C. L. Lundell, *Flora of Texas,* Vol. 3, Part 111, *Orchidaceae* by Donovan S. Correll, Dallas: Southern Methodist University, 1944; Geyata Ajilvsgi, *Wild Flowers of the Big Thicket*, Texas A&M University Press, 1979; and a list of Big Thicket wildflowers compiled by Geraldine Watson. Asterisks mark those species whose general distribution makes their existence in the Big Thicket area possible.

Wildflowers

Spring (March-April-May)

Entries in this index are taken from a list compiled by Geraldine Watson. Classifications are taken from Correll and Johnston, *Manual of the Vascular Plants of Texas,* Renner, Texas: Texas Research Foundation, 1970.

Beardtongue	*Penstemon laxiflorus*	Roadsides, Sand Woods
Bluebonnet	*Lupinus texensis*	Roadsides, Pastures
Swamp Buttercup	*Ranunculus septentrionalis*	Bottomlands
Dogwood	*Cornus florida*	Woods, Pine Uplands
Roughleaf Dogwood	*Cornus Drummondii*	Wetlands
Woodland Gerardia	*Gerardia aphylla*	Pastures, Sandy Woods
Green Dragon	*Arisaema dracontium*	Damp Woods
Horse Gentian	*Triosteum angustifolium*	Damp Pastures

Indian Paint Brush	*Castilleja indivisa*	Roadsides
Southern Blue Flag	*Iris virginica*	Marshes, Ditches
Yellow Iris	*Iris pseudacorys*	Marshes, Ditches
Spider Lily	*Hymenocallis liriosme*	Swamplands
Balespike Lobelia	*Lobelia spicata*	Roadsides
Varicolored Phlox	*Phlox drummondii*	Sandy Land
Ranunculus	*Ranunculus macranthus*	Damp Roadsides
Scarlet Pimpernel	*Anagallis arvensis*	Roadsides
Mock-orange	*Styrax americana*	Moist Woods
Azalea	*Rhododendron canescens*	Streambanks

Summer (June-July-August-September)

Wing-rib Sumac	*Rhus copallina*	Woods, Fencelines
St. Andrew's Cross	*Ascyrum hypericoides*	Pine Savannahs
Snow-on-the-mountain	*Euphorbia marginata*	Roadsides
Monkey-flower	*Mimulus alatus*	Streambottoms
Southern Swamp Lily	*Crinum americanum*	Brackish Swamps
Indian Plantain	*Cacalia lanceolata*	Acid Soils
Swamp Rose-Mallow	*Hibiscus moscheutos*	Wetlands
Tall Yellow Primrose	*Oenothera laciniata*	Roadsides, Sandy Fields
Elephant's Foot	*Elaphantopus nudatus*	Woodlands
Carolina-Lily	*Lilium michauxii*	Sandy Woods
Bunchflower	*Melanthium Virginicum*	Damp, Acid Woods
Bluebell Gentian	*Eustoma exaltatum*	Roadsides, Damp Fields
Bluecurls	*Trichostema dichotomum*	Sandy Soils
Blue Mistflower	*Eupatorium coelestinum*	Woods, Bottomlands
Wooly Croton	*Croton capitatus*	Fencelines, Prairies

Autumn (October-November)

Bottle Gentian	*Gentiana saponaria*	Bogs, Streambanks
Indian-Pipe	*Monotropa uniflora*	Moist Woodlands
Gay-Feather	*Liatris elegans*	Acid Soils
Southern Swamp Lily	*Crinum americanum*	Brackish Swamps

[203]

Black Nightshade	*Solanum americanum*	Streambanks, Thicket
Prairie Onion	*Allium stellatum*	Roadsides
Burmannia	*Burmannia biflora*	Acid Soils
Blackeyed Susan	*Rudbeckia hirta*	Roadsides
Lobelia	*Lobelia Reverchonii*	Bogs
Shadowwitch	*Ponthieva racemosa*	Streambanks

Winter (December-January-February)

Western Mayhaw	*Crataegus opaca*	Wetlands
Bluets	*Hedyotis australis*	Roadsides
Mayapple	*Podophyllum peltatum*	Woodlands
Sunnybells	*Schoenolirion croceum*	Acid Wetlands
Sunbonnets	*Chaptialia tomentosa*	Sandy Soils
Witch-Hazel	*Hamamelis virginiana*	Streambanks
Spring-Cress	*Cardamine bulbosa*	Bottomlands

Entries in this index are taken from a list compiled by Geraldine Watson. Classifications are taken from Correll and Johnston, *Manual of the Vascular Plants of Texas*. Renner, Texas: Texas Research Foundation, 1970.

Grasses

Redtop Bentgrass	*Agrostis stolonifera*
Autumn Bentgrass	*Agrostis perennans*
Hairgrass	*Aira elegans*
Foxtail	*Alopecurus carolinianus*
Little Bluestem	*Schizachyrum scoparium*
Arrowfeather	*Aristida purpurascens*
Giant Cane	*Arundinaria gigantea*
Georgia Cane	*Arundo Donax*
Carpet Grass	*Axonopus affinis*
Rescue Grass	Bromus unioloides
Ripgut Grass	Bromus rigidus

Field Sandbur	*Cenchrus incertus*
Poverty Oatgrass	*Danthonia spicata*
Crab Grass	*Digitaria sanguinalis*
Goosegrass	*Eleusine indica*
Wild-Rye	*Elymus canadensis*
Lacegrass	*Eragrostis capillaris*
Stinkgrass	*Eragrostis cilianensis*
Silver Plumegrass	*Erianthus alopecuriodes*
Sugarcane Plumegrass	*Erianthus giganteus*
Eastern Mannagrass	*Glyceria septentrionalis*
White Grass	*Leersia virginica*
Perennial Ryegrass	*Lolium perenne*
Witchgrass	*Panicum capillare*
Browntop Panic Grass	*Panicum fasciculatum*
Switchgrass	*Panium virgatum*
Knotgrass	*Paspalum distichum*
Annual Bluegrass	*Poa annua*
Kentucky Bluegrass	*Poa pratensis*
Indian Grass	*Sorghastrum avenaceum*
Blackseed Needlegrass	*Stipa avenacea*
Eastern Gamagrass	*Trypsacum dactyloides*
Southern Wildrice	*Zizaniopsis miliacea*
Yellow Nutgrass	*Cyperus esculentus*
Southern Nutgrass	*Cyperus rotundus*

This list was compiled from the *Biological Survey of the East Texas Big Thicket Area.*

Vines

Climbing Fern	*Lygodium japonicum*
Sarsparilla Vine	*Smilax pumila*
Laurel Green-brier	*Smilax laurifolia*
Saw-brier	*Smilax glauca*
Bullbrier	*Smilax Bona-nox*

China-root	*Smilax hispida*
Catbrier	*Smilax rotundifolia*
*Coral Green-brier	*Smilax Walteri*
Queen's Wreath	*Antigonon leptopus*
*Eardrop Vine	*Brunnichia ovata*
Clematis	*Clematis dioscoreifolia*
Virgin's-Bower	*Clematis virginiana*
Blue Jasmine	*Clematis crispa*
*Leather-Flower	*Clematis pitcheri*
Red-Berried Moonseed	*Cocculus carolinus*
Cupseed	*Calycocarpum Lyonii*
Climbing Rose	*Rosa setigera*
Wisteria	*Wisteria macrostachya*
*Dioclea	*Dioclea multiflora*
Poison Ivy	*Rhus toxicodendron*
Rattan-Vine	*Berchemia scandens*
Mustang Grape	*Vitis candicans*
Summer Grape	*Vitis aestivalis*
Muscadine	*Vitis rotundifolia*
Cat Grape	*Vitis palmata*
Fox Grape	*Vitis labrusca*
Virginia Creeper	*Parthenocissus quinquefolia*
Pepper-Vine	*Ampelopsis arborea*
Cross-Vine	*Bignonia capreolata*
Trumpet Honeysuckle	*Lonicera sempervirens*
Black-eyed Susan	*Thunbergia alata*
Japanese Honeysuckle	*Lonicera japonica*
Trumpet Honeysuckle	*Campsis radicans*
Bottle Gourd	*Lagenaria siceraria*
Wild Balsam-Apple	*Momordica Charantia*
*Climbing Hemp Vine	*Mikania scandens*

This list was compiled from D. S. Correll and M. C. Johnston, *Manual of the Vascular Plants of Texas*, Renner, Texas: Texas Research Foundation, 1970; and from H. B. Parks and V. L. Cory, *Biological Survey of the East Texas Big Thicket Area*. Plants rare in the Big Thicket are denoted by an asterisk.

Birds—Classification according to habitat

1. Marsh and water birds

Water-Turkey	*Anhinga anhinga*
*Wood Ibis	*Mycteria americana*
Roseate Spoonbill	*Ajaia ajaja*
**White-Faced Ibis	*Plegadis chihi*
**White Ibis	*Eudocimus albus*
Double-Crested Cormorant	*Phalacrocorax auritus*
**Olivaceous Cormorant	*Phalacrocorax olivaceus*
Great Blue Heron	*Ardea herodias*
Green Heron	*Butorides virescens*
Little Blue Heron	*Florida caerulea*
Louisiana Heron	*Hydranassa tricolor*
Black-Crowned Night Heron	*Nycticorax nycticorax*
Yellow-Crowned Night Heron	*Nyctanassa violacea*
Cattle Egret	*Bubulcis ibis*
American Egret	*Casmerodius albus*
Snowy Egret	*Egretta thula*
King Rail	*Rallus elegans*
Virginia Rail	*Rallus limicola*
Sora	*Porzana carolina*
*Purple Gallinule	*Porphyrula martinica*
Florida Gallinule	*Gallinula Chloropus*
American Coot	*Fulica americana*
*Least Bittern	*Ixobrychus exilis*
*American Bittern	*Botaurus lentiginosus*
xSandhill Crane	*Grus canadensis*
Fish Crow	*Corvus ossifragus*
*Fulvous Whistling-Duck	*Dendrocygna bicolor*
Wood Duck	*Aix sponsa*
*Canada Goose	*Branta canadensis*
*Snow Goose	*Chen caerulescens*

*Mallard	*Anas platyrhynchos*
*Pintail	*Anas acuta*
Blue-Winged Teal	*Anas discors*
*Shoveler	*Spatula clypeata*
*Redhead	*Aythya americana*
*Canvasback	*Aythya valisineria*

2. Thicket, baygall, dense undergrowth

*American Woodcock	*Scolopax minor*
xWinter Wren	*Troglodytes troglodytes*
**Brown Thrasher	*Toxostoma rufum*
White-eyed Vireo	*Vireo griseus*
*Prothonotary Warbler	*Protonotaria citrea*
xSwainson's Warbler	*Lymnothlypis swainsonii*
xBachman's Warbler	*Vermivora bachmanii*
*Ovenbird	*Seiurus aurocapillus*
*Northern Waterthrush	*Seiurus noveboracensis*
*Song Sparrow	*Melospiza melodia*

3. Pine woods

**Brown-Headed Nuthatch	*Sitta pusilla*
*Black-Throated Green Warbler	*Dendroica virens*
*Pine Warbler	*Dendroica pinus*
*Pine Siskin	*Carduelis pinus*
Bachman's Sparrow	*Aimophila aestivalis*
**Red-Cockaded Woodpecker	*Picoides borealis*
*Chuck-Will's Widow	*Caprimulgus carolinensis*

4. Savannahs, prairies, woods margins

*American Golden Plover	*Pluvialis dominica*
Roadrunner	*Geococcyx californianus*

Eastern Kingbird	*Tyrannus tyrannus*
*Scissor-tailed Flycatcher	*Tyrannus forficatus*
Mockingbird	*Mimus polyglottos*
*Eastern Bluebird	*Sialia sialis*
Loggerhead Shrike	*Lanius ludovicianus*
*Chestnut-Sided Warbler	*Dendroica pensylvanica*
xPrairie Warbler	*Dendroica discolor*
Eastern Meadowlark	*Sturnella magna*
*Indigo Bunting	*Passerina cyanea*
*Dickcissel	*Spiza americana*
*Savannah Sparrow	*Passerculus sanwichensis*
*Grasshopper Sparrow	*Ammodramus savannarum*
Lark Sparrow	*Chondestes grammacus*
*Yellow-Shafted Flicker	*Colaptes auratus*
Red-Headed Woodpecker	*Melanerpes erythrocephalus*

5. Hardwood and mixed pine-hardwood forests

Wild Turkey	*Meleagris gallopavo*
*Great Crested Flycatcher	*Myiarchus critinus*
Blue Jay	*Cyanocitta cristata*
Carolina Chickadee	*Parus carolinensis*
Tufted Titmouse	*Parus bicolor*
White-Breasted Nuthatch	*Sitta carolinensis*
*Yellow-Throated Vireo	*Vireo flavifrons*
*Solitary Vireo	*Vireo solitarius*
*Warbling Vireo	*Vireo gilvus*
*Parula Warbler	*Parula americana*
*Magnolia Warbler	*Dendroica magnolia*
*American Redstart	*Setophaga ruticilla*
*Scarlet Tanager	*Piranga olivacea*
*Whip-Poor-Will	*Caprimulgus vociferus*
Pileated Woodpecker	*Dryocopus pileatus*

Birds—Classification according to type

---

1. Predators

xWhite-Tailed Kite	*Elanus leucurus*
xSwallow-Tailed Kite	*Elanoides forficatus*
Eastern Red-Tailed Hawk	*Buteo jamaicencis borealis*
*Rough-Legged Hawk	*Buteo lagopus*
Florida Red-Shouldered Hawk	*Buteo lineatus alleni*
*Sharp-Shinned Hawk	*Accipiter striatus*
*Broad-Winged Hawk	*Buteo platypterus*
xMississippi Kite	*Ictinia misisippiensis*
*Cooper's Hawk	*Accipiter cooperii*
xHarlan's Hawk	*Buteo harlani*
xSwainson's Hawk	*Buteo swainsoni*
xGolden Eagle	*Aquila chrysaetos*
Bald Eagle	*Haliaeetus leucocephalus*
*Northern Harrier	*Circus cyaneus*
xOsprey	*Pandion haliaetus*
*Pigeon Hawk	*Falco columbarius*
American Kestrel	*Falco sparverius*
Peregrine Falcon	*Falco peregrinus*
Florida Barred Owl	*Strix varia alleni*
Great Horned Owl	*Bubo virginianus*
Florida Screech Owl	*Otus asoi horidanus*
*Short-Eared Owl	*Asio flammeus*
Barn Owl	*Tyto alba*
xSaw-Whet Owl	*Aegolius acadicus*
xLong-Eared Owl	*Asio otus*

2. Wood warblers

*Black and White Warbler	*Mniotilta varia*
*Prothonotary Warbler	*Protonotaria citrea*
xSwainson's Warbler	*Limnothlypis swainsoni*

xWorm-Eating Warbler	*Helmitheros vermivorus*
*Blue-Winged Warbler	*Vermivora pinus*
*Tennessee Warbler	*Vermivora peregrina*
*Orange-crowned Warbler	*Vermivora celata*
*Nashville Warbler	*Vermivora ruficapilla*
*Parula Warbler	*Parula americana*
*Yellow Warbler	*Dendroica petechia*
*Magnolia Warbler	*Dendroica magnolia*
xBlack-Throated Blue Warbler	*Dendroica caerulescens*
*Eastern Myrtle Warbler	*Dendroica coronata*
*Black-Throated Green Warbler	*Dendroica virens*
*Cerulean Warbler	*Dendroica cerulea*
*Blackburnian Warbler	*Dendroica fusca*
*Yellow-Throated Warbler	*Dendroica dominica*
*Chestnut-Sided Warbler	*Dendroica pensylvanica*
*Bay-Breasted Warbler	*Dendroica castanea*
xBlackpoll Warbler	*Dendroica striata*
*Pine Warbler	*Dendroica pinus*
xPalm Warbler	*Dendroica palmarum*
*Ovenbird	*Seiurus aurocapillus*
*Northern Waterthrush	*Seiurus noveboracensis*
*Louisiana Waterthrush	*Seiurus motacilla*
*Kentucky Warbler	*Oporornis formosus*
xConnecticut Warbler	*Oporornis agilis*
*Mourning Warbler	*Oporornis philadelphia*
*Yellowthroat	*Goethlypis trichas*
*Yellow-Breasted Chat	*Icteria virens*
*Hooded Warbler	*Wilsonia citrina*
*Wilson's Warbler	*Wilsonia pusilla*
*Canada Warbler	*Wilsonia canadensis*
*American Redstart	*Setophaga ruticilla*
xBachman's Warbler	*Vermivora bachmanii*

3. Sparrows

*Savannah Sparrow	*Passerculus sandwichensis*
*Grasshopper Sparrow	*Ammodramus savannarum*
*LeConte's Sparrow	*Ammodramus leconteii*
*Henslow's Sparrow	*Ammodramus henslowii*
**Sharp-Tailed Sparrow	*Ammodramus caudacutus*
*Vesper Sparrow	*Pooecetes gramineus*
Lark Sparrow	*Chondestes grammacus*
Bachman's Sparrow	*Aimophila aestivalis*
*Chipping Sparrow	*Spizella passerina*
xClay-Colored Sparrow	*Spizella pallida*
Field Sparrow	*Spizella pusilla*
*Harris Sparrow	*Zonotrichia querula*
*White-Crowned Sparrow	*Zonotrichia leucophrys*
*White-Throated Sparrow	*Zonotrichia albicollis*
*Fox Sparrow	*Passerella iliaca*
*Lincoln's Sparrow	*Melospiza lincolnii*
*Swamp Sparrow	*Melospiza georgiana*
*Song Sparrow	*Melospiza melodia*
House Sparrow	*Passer domesticus*

4. Woodpeckers

*Yellow-Shafted Flicker	*Colaptes auratus*
*Red-Shafted Flicker	*Colaptes cafer*
*Ivory-Billed Woodpecker	*Campephilus principalis* (extinct)
Pileated Woodpecker	*Dryocopus pileatus*
Red-bellied Woodpecker	*Melanerpes carolinus*
Red-Headed Woodpecker	*Melanerpes erythrocephalus*
*Yellow-Bellied Sapsucker	*Sphyrapicus varius*
Hairy Woodpecker	*Picoides villosus*
Downy Woodpecker	*Picoides pubescens*
**Red-Cockaded Woodpecker	*Picoides borealis*

5. Rare or scarce birds

**Brown-Headed Nuthatch	*Sitta pusilla*
Peregrine Falcon	*Falco peregrinus*
**Red-Cockaded Woodpecker	*Picoides borealis*
xSwainson's Warbler	*Lymothlypis swainsonii*
**Wood Duck	*Aix sponsa*
xWhite-Tailed Kite	*Elanus leucrus*
xSwallow-Tailed Kite	*Elanoides forficatus*
xMississippi Kite	*Ictinia misisippiensis*
xBachman's Warbler	*Vermivora bachmanii*
xLeConte's Sparrow	*Ammondramus leconteii*
xGolden Eagle	*Aquila chrysaetos*
xBald Eagle	*Haliaeetus leucocephalus*

Most of the categories in this list are incomplete. Possible exceptions are the warblers and woodpeckers. Only those sparrows are listed which bear the word "sparrow" in their title; additions to the list of sparrows are therefore possible. The White-Tailed Kite was identified by the author in the Big Thicket in the spring of 1971.

The classification of a species under a given habitat does not imply that it can not be found elsewhere. Classification according to both habitat and type results inevitably in some duplications from list to list.

An asterisk (*) to the left of an entry signifies that it is migratory. Two asterisks (**) signify that it is rarely or infrequently seen in the Big Thicket. An "x" signifies that it is both migratory and rarely or infrequently seen.

This list has been compiled from several sources. Among these are: Mrs. C. H. Newsom and Mrs. Lynette McGaugh, "Spring Count 1967 May 4, Evadale, Village Mills, Hillister, Kountze and surrounding areas in Hardin, Jasper and Tyler Counties"; Mrs. Charles H. Newsom, compiler, "Spring Bird Count 1968 April 28, Hardin, Tyler, Jasper and Liberty Counties"; Mrs. Cleve Bachman, personal correspondence, September, 1970; Roger Tory Peterson, *A Field Guide to the Birds of Texas*, Boston:

Houghton Mifflin Company, 1963; Olin Sewall Pettingill, Jr., *A Guide to Bird Finding West of the Mississippi*, New York: Oxford University Press, 1953; James Cassidy, *Book of North American Birds*, Pleasantville, New York: Reader's Digest Association, 1990.

Reptiles

Alligator	*Alligator mississippiensis*
Chameleon	*Anolis carolinensis*
East Texas Sand Lizard	*Holbrookia propinqua propinqua*
Horned Toad	*Phrynosoma cornutum*
Pine Lizard	*Sceloporus undulatus undulatus*
Glass Snake	*Opisaurus ventralis*
Stripped Racehorse Lizard	*Cnemidophorus sexlineatus*
Bluetailed Skink	*Eumeces fasciatus*
Worm Snake	*Carphophis amena vermis*
Yellowbelly Racer	*Coluber constrictor flaviventris*
Tan Racer	*Coluber constrictor etheridgei*
Ringneck Snake	*Diadophis punctatus arnyi*
Rat Snake	*Elaphe obsoleta lindheimerei*
Western Pine Snake	*Thamnophis proximus*
Mud Snake	*Farancia abacura*
Hognose Snake	*Heterodon platyrhinos*
Yellow-bellied King Snake	*Lampropeltis calligaster*
Speckled King Snake	*Lampropeltis getulus*
Milk Snake	*Lampropeltis triangulum*
Coach Whip	*Masticophis flagellum flagellum*

Southern Water Snake	*Nerodia fasciata*
Plainbelly Water Snake	*Nerodia erythrogaster*
Green Water Snake	*Nerodia cyclopion*
Diamondback Water Snake	*Nerodia rhombifera*
Ringneck Snake	*Diadophis punctatus*
Louisiana Pine Snake	*Pituophis melanoleucus ruthveni*
Brown Snake	*Storeria dekayi*
Flathead Snake	*Tantilla gracilis*
Garter Snake	*Thamnophis sirtalis sirtalis*
Lined Snake	*Tropidoclonion lineatum*
*Coral Snake	*Micrurus fulvius fulvius*
*Copperhead	*Agkistrodon contortrix contortrix*
*Cottonmouth Moccasin	*Agkistrodon piscivorus*
*Canebrake Rattler	*Crotalus horridus atricaudatus*
*Timber Rattlesnake	*Crotalus horridus horridus*
*Ground Rattler	*Sistrurus miliarus miliarus*
Mississippi Mud Turtle	*Kinosternon subrubrum*
Keeled Mud Turtle	*Sternotherus carinatus*
Southern Musk Turtle	*Sternotherus odoratus*
Snapping Turtle	*Chelydra serpentina*
Alligator Snapping Turtle	*Macrochclemys temminckii*
Gopher Tortoise	*Gopherus polyphemus*
Eastern Box Turtle	*Terrapene carolina*
Smooth Soft-shelled Turtle	*Trionyx muticus*

This list is compiled from the *Biological Survey of the East Texas Big Thicket* and R. E. Ballinger and J. D. Lynch, *How to Know the Amphibians and Reptiles*, Dubuque, Iowa: Wm. C. Brown, 1983. An asterisk denotes a poisonous snake.

Mammals

Florida Opossum	*Didelphis virginiana*
*Black Bear	*Ursus americanus*
Raccoon	*Procyon lotor fuscipes*
*Ringtail	*Bassariscus astutus*
Mink	*Mustela vison*
River Otter	*Lutra canadensis*
Gulf Spotted Skunk	*Spilogale putorius*
Striped Skunk	*Memphitus mephitus*
Red Fox	*Vulpes vulpes*
Florida Gray Fox	*Urocyon cinereoargenteus floridanus*
*Coyote	*Canis latrans*
*Texas Red Wolf	*Canis rufus*
*Panther	*Felis concolor*
Texas Bobcat	*Felis rufus*
Fox Squirrel	*Sciurus niger*
Grey Squirrel	*Sciurus carolinensis*
Flying Squirrel	*Glaucomys volans*
Beaver	*Castor canadensis*
Muskrat	*Ondatra zibethicus*
Cottontail Rabbit	*Sylvilagus floridanus alacer*
Swamp Rabbit	*Sylvilagus aquaticus*
Whitetailed Deer	*Odocoileus Virginianus texanus*
Nine-banded Armadillo	*Dasypus novemcinctus texanus*

This list was compiled from the *Biological Survey of the East Texas Big Thicket Area* and William B. Davis, *The Mammals of Texas*, Austin, Texas: Texas Parks and Wildlife Department, 1966. Asterisks indicate that a species is rare in the Big Thicket.

The entries in this appendix are not intended to be complete; they are intended to display the general nature of the life of the Big Thicket.

Bibliography

Francis Edward Abernethy, *Tales From The Big Thicket*, Austin: University of Texas Press, 1966.

Geyata Ajilvsgi, *Wild Flowers of the Big Thicket*, College Station and London: Texas A & M University Press, 1979.

Ruth A. Allen, *East Texas Lumber Workers, An Economic and Social Picture, 1870-1950*, Austin: University of Texas Press, 1961.

Orrin H. Bonney, "Big Thicket Biological Crossroads of North America," *The Living Wilderness*, 33, No. 106, Summer 1969, 19-21.

William T. Chambers, "Divisions of the Pine Forest Belt of East Texas," *Economic Geography*, 10, No. 3, July 1934, 302-18.

James Joseph Cozine, "Assault on a Wilderness: The Big Thicket of East Texas," Ph.D. dissertation, Texas A & M University, August, 1976.

Carlton C. Curtis and S. C. Bausor, *The Complete Guide to North American Trees*, New York: Collier Books, 1943.

William B. Davis, *The Mammals of Texas*, Austin, Texas: Texas Parks and Wildlife Department, 1966.

William O. Douglas, *Farewell to Texas, A Vanishing Wilderness*, New York: McGraw-Hill Book Company, 1967.

Dennis Farney, "Deciding on a 'Last True Wilderness,'" *Wall Street Journal*, July 1, 1968, 12.

W. E. S. Folsom-Dickerson, *The White Path*, 2nd Printing, San Antonio, Texas: The Naylor Company, 1965.

Michael S. Fountain and R. Lee Rayburn, *Impact of Oil/Gas Development on Vegetation and Soils of Big Thicket National Preserve,* (National Park Service Cooperative Park Studies Unit, Texas A & M University, March 1, 1987. Technical Report No. 5).

"Geological Whodunit," *The Texaco Star,* Fall 1946, 22-3.

Ray Gill, "The Big Thicket of East Texas," *Beaumont Business*, May 1938.

James C. Greenway, *Extinct and Vanishing Birds of the World*, 2nd ed., New York: Dover Publications, Inc., 1957.

William P. Gregg, Jr. and Betsy Ann McGean, "Biosphere Reserves: Their History and Their Promise," *Orion Nature Quarterly*, 4, No. 3, Summer 1985, 41-51.

William Carey Grimm, *The Book of Trees*, Harrisburg, Pennsylvania, 1962.

Ludlow Griscom and Alexander Sprunt, *The Warblers of America*, New York: The Devin-Adair Company, 1957.

John A. Haislet, "National Champion Trees of Texas," Circular 86, Texas Forest Service, November 1964.

Leon Augustus Hausman, *The Illustrated Encyclopedia of American Birds,* Garden City, New York: Garden City Publishing Company, Inc., 1947.

Dempsie Henley, *The Big Thicket Story*, Waco: Texian Press, 1967.

_____, *The Murder of Silence*, Waco: Texian Press, 1970.

Ed Holder, "Pocketful of Squirrels," *Texas Game and Fish*, 22, No. 1, January 1966, 4-5, 30.

Romeyn Beck Hough, *Handbook of the Trees of the Northern States and Canada*, Lowville, New York: Published by the author, 1907.

Ted Killian, "The Big Thicket of East Texas: A Study in the Process of Preservation," Submitted to Professor Manners for GRG 388, Austin, Texas, April 1991, 36.

Lamar State College of Technology, School of Education, *A Unit of the Big Thicket for Use on Sixth Grade Level*, Beaumont: Lamar State College of Technology, 1963.

Mary Lasswell, *I'll Take Texas*, Boston: Houghton Mifflin Company, 1958.

Gideon Lincecum, "Journal," Manuscript #1263, University of Texas Archives.

Cyrus Longworth Lundell, ed., *Contributions from the Texas Research Foundation*, 1, Part 3, "The Oaks of Texas," by Cornelius H. Muller, Renner, Texas: Texas Research Foundation, 1951.

Claude A. McLeod, "The Big Thicket Forest of East Texas," *The Texas Journal of Science*, 23, No. 2, November 1971, 221-33.

————, *The Big Thicket of East Texas*, Huntsville, Texas: The Sam Houston Press, 1967.

Frank Morris and Edward A. Eames, *Our Wild Orchids*, New York: Charles Scribner's Sons, 1929.

Frederick Law Olmstead, *A Journey Through Texas*, New York: Dix, Edwards & Co., 1857.

Lois Williams Parker, *Big Thicket Bibliography,* Saratoga, Texas: Big Thicket Museum, 1970. (Big Thicket Museum Publication Series, No. 2)

H. B. Parks, "The Big Thicket," *Texas Geographic Magazine*, 2, No. 1, Summer 1938, 16-28.

_____, "The Biogeography of East Texas" (Abstract), *Proceedings and Transactions of the Texas Academy of Science*, 23, 1942, 42.

_____, "Research in Biotic Zones in Texas" (Abstract), *Proceedings and Transactions of the Texas Academy of Science*, 23, 1938-1939, 43-44.

_____, V. L. Cory and others, *Biological Survey of the East Texas Big Thicket Area*, 2d Edition, 1938.

Wilbur F. Pate, "The Logging Industry at Diboll, Texas," *Proceedings and Transactions of the Texas Academy of Science*, 28, 1944, 232-41.

Howard Peacock, *The Big Thicket of Texas: America's Ecological Wonder*, Foreword by Francis Edward Abernethy, Boston: Little, Brown and Company, 1984.

Roger Tory Peterson, *A Field Guide to the Birds of Texas*, Boston: Houghton Mifflin Company, 1963.

Olin Sewall Pettingill, *A Guide to Bird Finding West of the Mississippi*, New York: Oxford University Press, 1953.

Linda Gable Pierce, "The Future of the Big Thicket of Texas," Master's thesis, The University of Texas at Austin, 1972.

Caleb Pirtle III, "The Fight to Save Our Land and Heritage," *Southern Living*, 5, No. 3, May 1970, 48-9.

Richard J. Preston, Jr., *North American Trees*, Cambridge, Massachusetts: The M.I.T. Press, 1966.

Proposed Big Thicket National Monument, Texas, A Study of Alternatives, National Park Service, United States Department of the Interior, February 1967.

Mark D. Rausher, "Search Image For Leaf Shape in a Butterfly," *Science*, 200, No. 4345, 2 June 1978, 1071-73.

Franklin M. Reck, "Big Thicket," *Frontier Times*, March 1949, 39-43.

James Robert Reed, "Preservation Management in the Big Thicket," Master's thesis, The University of Texas at Austin, 1979.

Harold William Rickett, *Wild Flowers of the United States*, 1, Part Two, The Southeastern States, New York: McGraw-Hill, 1967. (The Orchid Family, 94-130)

Berton Roueché, "The Witness Tree," *The New Yorker*, August 31, 1968, 56-64.

Robert C. Scase and Clifford J. Martinka, eds. *Towards the Biosphere Reserve: Exploring Relationships Between Parks and Adjacent Lands*. Proceedings of an International Symposium, Kalispell, Montana, June 22-24, 1982. Published by United States Department of the Interior, National Park Service, 1983.

David J. Schmidly, with William G. Norton and Gail A. Barber, *The Game and Furbearing Mammals of Big Thicket National Preserve With Comments on the Small Fauna of Selected Units*, Santa Fe, New Mexico, September, 1980.

Ellen D. Schulz and Robert Runyon, *Texas Cacti*, San Antonio: Texas Academy of Science, 1930.

Harry J. Shafer, Edward P. Baxter, Thomas B. Stearns, and James Phil Dering, *An Archaeological Assessment of the Big Thicket National Preserve*, Anthropological Laboratory, Texas A & M University, October 1975. (Report No. 19)

Emma Mae Smelley, "Polk County, Texas—A Geographic Survey," *The Texas Geographic Magazine*, 9, No. 1, Spring 1945, 15-21.

Royal D. Suttkus and Glenn H. Clemmer, *The Fishes of Big Thicket National Preserve*, n.d. (*circa* 1980).

Benjamin Carroll Tharp, *Structure of Texas Vegetation East of the 98th Meridian*, Austin: University of Texas Press, 1926. (University of Texas Bulletin No. 2606)

UNESCO, *Task Force on: Criteria and Guidelines for the Choice and Establishment of Biosphere Reserves*, MAB Report Series No. 22, Unesco, Paris, 1974.

Geraldine Watson, *Big Thicket Plant Ecology: An Introduction*, Saratoga, Texas: Big Thicket Museum, 1975. (Big Thicket Museum Publication Series, No. 5)

_____, *Vegetative Survey of the Big Thicket National Preserve*, 1982, 160.

Joe Cauker Wells, "Environmental Interest Groups: A Case Study, The Big Thicket Association," Master's thesis, University of Texas at Arlington, 1981.

L. R. Wolfe, *Check-list of the Birds of Texas*, Lancaster, Pennsylvania: Intelligencer Printing Company, 1956.

Solomon Alexander Wright, *My Rambles*, Arrangement and Introduction by J. Frank Dobie, Austin: Texas Folklore Society, 1942.

Index

Abernethy, Francis Edward ("Ab"), 41, 55–56
Allred, James, 67
Alma Drive, 164
American Institute of Mining Engineers, 10–11
Anderson, Texas, 184
Arid Sandland Area, 102, 132
Audubon Society, 61
Austroriparian Province, 107
Baird, Donald O., 70
Batson, Texas, 9, 121
Baylor University, 175
Beaumont, Texas, 55, 62, 65, 80, 92, 148, 154, 155, 164, 165
Beaumont Enterprise, 69
Chamber of Commerce, 68
Beech-Magnolia Canyons, 184
Bentsen, Lloyd, 85, 92, 93, 95, 96, 97, 99, 175
Best Use Policy, 182–83
Bevil Oaks, 166
Bible, Allan, 83
bicycling, 139
Big Pine Island Bayou, 41
Big Thicket
Addition Bill, 109–10, 175–79
Associations, 67–73, 78, 95, 96–97
Biological Survey, 14, 37
Coordinating Committee, 88, 91, 92, 95, 97
geology, 44–46, 148–50
location, 39–51
mapping, 37–38, 75, 100
maps, 42–43, 87, 112–13
Museum, 146, 179
National Monument, 61, 76
National Park, 47, 67, 69, 73–75, 83, 85–86, 92
National Preserve, 97, 100, 105, 119, 168, 170, 176–79, 184, 188
Profile, 49, 61, 78, 86
soil types, 38
State Forest, 72
Visitors Information Center, 124, 128, 135, 179
Big Thicket Units
Beaumont Unit, 49, 50, 148, 166
Beech Creek, 49, 50, 61, 76, 88, 114, 143–46
Big Sandy Creek, 95, 102, 108, 109, 137–43
Big Sandy-Village Creek Corridor, 93, 95, 96, 102, 108, 109, 175, 176
Canyonlands, 109
Cypress Creek, 76

Hickory Creek Savannah, 49,
50, 134–136
Jack Gore Baygall, 148–56,
189
Lance Rosier, 114, 115–19,
147, 168, 175
Loblolly, 49, 50, 61, 121
Lower Neches River Corridor,
95, 108, 109, 147–55, 189
Menard Creek Corridor, 122–
24, 168
Neches Bottom, 49, 50, 148,
153
Neches Corridor, 102
Pine Island Bayou, 78, 147,
164–66, 172, 175
Tanner Bayou, 49, 168
Turkey Creek, 95, 102, 108,
109, 124–34, 158, 159, 187–
88
Black Creek Road, 175
Blue Hole, 3
bogs, 49, 119, 131, 134
Borgman, Ernest, 58–60
Bowmer, Jim, 73
Bridges, Edwin, 103
Brooks, Jack, 88, 92
Brotherhood of Timber Workers,
8
burnouts, 3, 7
Bush, George W., 86
Cabell, Earl, 86, 88
Calder Lane, 165
canoeing, 147–58
Carter Lumber Company, 143
Carter Sand and Water Stop,
184
Champion International, 182,
184–85
Church House Road, 119

Connally, John, 72
conservation, 53–65, 67–84,
147, 167–91
conservationists, 64, 72, 75, 78,
80, 82, 85, 180, 184
Cornell University, 146
Correll, Donovan, 40
Corrigan, Texas, 184
Cottam, Clarence, 73
Cotten family, 62, 116
Cotten Road, 62, 115–16, 118
County Line Road, 124, 127
Cozine, James J., 91, 93
Crawford, Ollie R., 82–83
creeks
Alabama, 39
Batiste, 184
Beech, 143–46, 168
Big Sandy, 50, 109, 137–143
Cypress, 158
Dillard, 184
Hickory, 135–36, 168
Kickapoo, 184
Kinky Branch, 115
Little Cypress Creek, 49
Long King, 184
Menard, 50, 122, 124
Turkey, 132, 135, 158
Village, 83, 101, 102, 103,
109, 110, 130, 156–58, 159,
168, 172
Vincent, 184
White Rock, 184
Crockett, Texas, 184
Dallardsville, Texas, 139
dams, 108, 109, 150, 152, 153,
155
Daniel, Bill, 71
Daniel, Price, 71, 72, 168
Dannemeyer, William, 177